Multiple Choice Questions in LIBRARY AND INFORMATION SCIENCE

(For NET/SET/SLET and Other Competitive Examinations)

By
Deepmala Nigam

Ess Ess Publications
New Delhi

Multiple Choice Questions in Library and Information Science
(For NET/ SET/ SLET and Other Competitive Examinations)

ISBN: 978-81-7000-731-9

₹ 950/-

First Published 2014

Published by:
Ess Ess Publications
4831/24, Ansari Road,
Darya Ganj,
New Delhi-110 002.
INDIA
Phones: 23260807, 41563444
Fax: 41563334
E-mail: info@essessreference.com
www.essessreference.com

Cover Design by *Patch Creative Unit*

Printed and bound in India at Salasar Imaging Systems.

dedicated to
The Memory of
my Late Father
SHRI B.B.L. SAXENA

Contents

Preface

After clearing UP-SLET, UGC-NET, and Ph.D. entrance CET-2012 conducted by Faizabad University, Faizabad (U.P.), I thought it prudent to share this knowledge with aspirants in shape of the book in hand for a large number of professionals who are trying to succeed in various State and National level examinations such as NET/SET/SLET/JRF/SSB and many other competitive exams such as Kendreya Vidyalaya Sangathan, Navodaya etc. I have made sincere efforts to share all I learnt with the readers and feel that this book shall be a value addition in the readers' bank of knowledge

Besides basics of the subject, I have made all efforts to incorporate all the latest and emerging concepts which are necessary for every aspirant to grasp and understand in depth for cracking the competitive examination they are appearing for. Though I have tried my best to give authentic and reliable information, but in case of any inadvertent error I apologize in advance. Suggestions from the readers shall tell me where I need to work harder and they are most welcome. Readers' valuable feedback shall help me improve the future editions of this book.

1

Universe of Knowledge and Information Processing

(1) Classification Word Originated from

(a) Greek Word (b) Latin Word

(c) Roman Word (d) French Word

(2) The classification based on

(a) Process of good and bad

(b) Process of grouping like entities & unlike entities

(c) Process of notation

(d) Process of random selection

(3) Who said "Library Classification is the arrangement of books on shelves or description of them in the manner which is most useful to those who read"

(a) WC Berwick Sayers (b) Margrett Mann

(c) Hulme (d) Robertson

(4) Classificatory language consists

(a) Hindi alphabets (b) Digits and symbols

(c) Spoken language (d) Braile script

(5) Match the following

(a)	Book classification	(i)	One who devise scheme of classification
(c)	Depth classification	(ii)	Classification of Macro subject
(b)	Ultimate class	(iii)	Classification of micro subject
(d)	Classificationist	(iv)	Smallest extension of a class

	A	B	C	D
(a)	I	II	III	IV
(b)	II	I	IV	III
(c)	IV	I	III	II
(d)	II	III	IV	I

(6) Version 2 of colon classification consists of

(a) CC 1, CC 2nd, CC 3rd ed

(b) CC 4th, CC5th, CC 6th and 6th revised with annexure

(c) CC 4th, CC 5th, CC 6th

(d) CC 5th, CC 6th , CC 7th editions.

(7) A subject with smallest extension and great intension is known as

(a) Macro subject (b) Spot subject

(c) Micro subject (d) Main class in CC

(8) Oldest scheme of Library classification is

(a) LC (b) SC

(c) DDC (d) UDC

(9) Library of congress classification and Rider's International classification are the examples of-

(a) Enumerative classification

(b) Almost enumerative classification

(c) Almost faceted classification

(d) Rigidly faceted classification

(10) In CC 7th edition Notation for Pakistan is

(a) 44Q7 (b) 44 T

(c) 44 X (d) 44Q71

(11) The five laws of Library science were first formulated in the year

(a) 1924 (b) 1928

(c) 1931 (d) 1933

(12) The connecting symbol for time facet (.) dot was replaced by (') single inverted comma in the year

(a) 1939 (b) 1954

(c) 1954 (d) 1963

(13) From the following which is not a quality of notation according to Dr Ranganathan ?

(a) Brief (b) Common

(c) Pronounceable (d) Simplicity

(14) The subject of Mathematics in CC give rise to Arithmetic, Algebra, Analysis, Trigonometry by following the

(a) Principle of later in time

(b) Principle of decreasing extension

(c) Principle of canonical sequence

(d) Principle of increasing intension

(15) In CC 6th edition the Notation HX represents the class

(a) Geology (b) Biology

(c) Animal Husbandry (d) Mining

(16) If the book number for 4th copy of same subject same class is N69;3 what will be the book number for 1st copy

(a) N69.1 (b) N69;1

(c) N69 (d) N69;2

(17) In five fundamental categories which category does not have levels?

(a) Personality (b) Matter

(c) Energy (d) None of the above

(18) APUPA pattern was designed by

(a) W.C. Berwick Sayers (b) Dr. S.R. Ranganathan

(c) C.A.cutter (d) A. Panizzi

(19) Who is the author of Prolegomena?

(a) Eugiene Garfield (b) Melvil Dewey

(c) KC Marrison (d) S.R. Ranganathan

(20) Which one award is given to Dr. S.R. Ranganathan by govt. of India?

(a) Padam Bhushan (b) Padam Shree

(c) Arjun Award (d) Literacy Award

(21) Relate the following schemes of classification with their origin year

(a)	The Bibliographic Classification	(i)	1905
(b)	Subject classification	(ii)	1933
(c)	Colon classification	(iii)	1935
(d)	Universal decimal classification	(iv)	1906

	A	**B**	**C**	**D**
(a)	I	II	III	IV
(b)	II	III	IV	I
(c)	III	IV	II	I
(d)	I	IV	II	III

(22) UDC is Based on Dewey decimal classification scheme. It used DDC -

(a) 1st Edition (b) II edition

(c) IVth Edition (d) Vth Edition

(23) The scheme for classification consists of large schedule of enumerated subject of past, present and anticipated future with the schedule of common

isolate

(a) Almost enumerative scheme

(b) Almost faceted scheme

(c) Purely enumerative scheme

(d) Freely faceted scheme

(24) Universal Decimal classification scheme is an example of

(a) Enumerative scheme of classification

(b) Almost enumerative scheme of classification

(c) Almost faceted scheme of classification

(d) Almost freely faceted scheme of classification

(25) CC 1 edition to 3rd edition was based on

(a) Enumerative scheme of classification

(b) Rigidly faceted scheme of classification

(c) Almost faceted scheme of classification

(d) Freely faceted scheme of classification

(26) Prolegomena IIIrd ed, book written by Dr. Ranganathan based on the

(a) Descriptive Theory (b) Dynamic Theory

(c) Static Theory (d) Both a+b

(27) Canons for helpful sequence are found at

(a) Idea plane

(b) National plane

(c) Verbal plane

(d) Idea plane and verbal plane

(28) DDC 22 edition consists of 6 tables excluding

(a) Table 6 (b) Table 3

(c) Table 4 (d) Table 7

(29) Common Auxiliary of point of view is found in

(a) DDC (b) UDC

(c) CC (d) LC

(30) In UDC = (equal) sign is used before

(a) Common Auxiliary of time

(b) Common Auxiliary of Language

(c) Common Auxiliary of form

(d) Common Auxiliary of space

(31) Compose the classification scheme with their Author

(a)	Expensive classification	(i)	Paul Outlet and Henry La Fontaine
(b)	Subject classification	(ii)	Charles Amie Cutter
(c)	Bibliographic classification	(iii)	James Duff Broun
(d)	Universal Decimal classification	(iv)	H.E. Bliss

	A	B	C	D
(a)	II	III	IV	III
(b)	IV	III	II	I
(c)	II	IV	III	I
(d)	II	IV	I	III

(32) In CC same concept represented by notation 4 in Biological Science for Disease, in sociology for social pathology and in law for tort It implies

(a) Scheduled mnemonics

(b) Seminal mnemonics

(c) Systematic mnemonics

(d) Alphabetical mnemonics

(33) In facet sequence which facet should come first in facet sequence if following" is whole organ principal"

(a) Term denoting whole

(b) Term denoting organ

(c) Term denoting classification

(d) None of the above

(34) Cow and calf principle implies in facet sequence

(a) Keep both facet in same round

(b) Keep one facet only one round

(c) Keep both facet at one level

(d) Keep both facet in different round

(35) 'Treatment of disease' is two facet of different round. Which principle is followed in their sequence

(a) Cow and Calf principle

(b) Whole organ principle

(c) Wall picture principle

(d) None of the above

(36) Complete the name of the principle of facet sequence starting with Actand

(a) Action – Actor-Tool

(b) Act-Action Actor

(c) Actors – Actions tools

(d) Tool – Act- Acting

(37) It is a type of mnemonics in which same concept, same term, is represent by same notation the subject may be in classification. It is called

(a) Scheduled mnemonics

(b) Seminal mnemonics

(c) Systematic mnemonics

(d) Alphabetical mnemonics

(38) Name the person who regarded as the first person made an attempt to set down a theory of classification

(a) S.R. Ranganathan (b) D.J. Foskett

(c) E.R. Richardson (d) Hulme

(39) Area study, generalia person study and study of entity are give rise subject/subjects under the mode of formation

(a) Lamination (b) Agglomeration
(c) Clustering (d) Fission

(40) In 1950, S.R. Ranganathan founded —— in Delhi
(a) Library research circle
(b) Library research group
(c) Library and research
(d) None of the above

(41) CRG was founded in this city
(a) New York (b) New Delhi
(c) Columbia (d) London

(42) Which of the following scheme was devised by corporate body
(a) BC (b) LC
(c) EC (d) CC

(43) In CC Forming a class no, two or more isolate of the same array in a facet are taken together by using
(a) Gap device
(b) Subject device
(c) Superimposition device
(d) Alphabetical device

(44) Backward arrow and Forward arrow are the indicator digits used in
(a) DDC (b) UDC
(c) CC (d) None of the above

(45) Sinology is the study of
(a) Japan (b) Singapore
(c) China (d) Bhutan

(46) (L) (F) (Y) (AN), (V) etc are related to
(a) Class number
(b) Collection number
(c) Biscoe Book Number
(d) Ranganathan Book Number

(47) In CC collection No for the document of abnormal size is written by

(a) Under line the Book No.

(b) Over line the Book No.

(c) Under line and over line the Book No.

(d) By writing AB

(48) Dissections and denudation are related to

(a) Fusion (b) Agglomeration

(c) Lamination (d) Fission

(49) Research Methodology subject is the result of which one of the following Modes of formation

(a) Loose Assemblage (b) Lamination

(c) Distillation (d) Clustering

(50) Loose Assemblage Kind 2 gives rise to

(a) Inter subject phase relation

(b) Intra facet phase relation

(c) Intra array phase relation

(d) None of the above

(51) Partial comprehension, a mode of formation of subject now known as

(a) Agglomeration (b) Cluster

(c) Distillation (d) Fission

(52) DDC 23rd edition was published in

(a) 2010 (b) 2011

(c) 2012 (d) 2013

(53) Now DDC 23rd Ed contains 6 table instead of 7 which one is not added as a table

(a) Table of subdivision individual language

(b) Table of Area

(c) Table of Language

(d) Table of Persons.

(54) DDC is an

(a) Enumerated Scheme

(b) Almost enumerative

(c) Almost faceted

(d) Almost freely faceted

(55) In DDC table 3 is known as

(a) Individual subdivision of languages

(b) Individual subdivision of literature

(c) Racial Ethnic National groups

(d) Languages

(56) The division of knowledge at every step must be into two. This process known as

(a) Polychotomy (b) Dichotomy

(c) Decachotomy (d) Proliferation

(57) Who said "Universe of Subject is a turbulent ever growing dynamic continuum"

(a) EJ coats (b) Plamer

(c) S.R. Ranganathan (d) Melvil Dewey

(58) In this form of catalogue each leaf contains six entries

(a) Guard book catalogue

(b) Loose leaf catalogue

(c) Print catalogue

(d) Co-operative catalogue

(59) In the following which is not a physical form of catalogue

(a) Printed book form (b) Sheaf catalogue

(c) Seat catalogue (d) General book catalogue

(60) Inner forms of the catalogue means

(a) Card catalogue

(b) Bibliographical information

(c) Physical forms

(d) Order in which entries are arranged in the catalogue

(61) Which catalogue has names of the persons as subject

(a) Author catalogue (b) Title catalogue

(c) Name catalogue (d) None of the above

(62) If the catalogue arrange all entries as author, title, subject, series etc in one alphabetical sequence it is called

(a) Dictionary catalogue

(b) Alphabetical subject catalogue

(c) Alphabetical – classed catalogue

(d) Classified catalogue

(63) Collaborator entry does not contain name of .... as heading

(a) Author (b) Reviser

(c) Translator (d) Editor

(64) In CCC cross-reference entry is also known as

(a) Main entry

(b) Number entry

(c) Cross reference Index entry

(d) None of the above

(65) In case of pseudonym we refer user to pseudonym to real name or real name to pseudonym with the help of

(a) CRIE (b) CRE

(c) CIE (d) BIE

(66) How many levels of description has prepared by AACR2 for main entry?

(a) One level of description

(b) Three levels of description
(c) Two levels of description
(d) Four levels of description

(67) Library of congress list of subject heading was first published in
(a) 1919 (b) 1909
(c) 1901 (d) None of the above

(68) Sears list of subject heading is devised by
(a) Alexandria (b) Naine E Browne
(c) Minnie Earl (d) Margaret Mann

(69) Cataloguing in source implies
(a) Cataloguing in library
(b) Entries are made co-operatively
(c) Entries are made in book itself
(d) None of the above

(70) Pre-natal cataloguing mean
(a) Cataloguing of book before their publications come in market
(b) Cataloguing of book by librarian
(c) Cataloguing
(d) Freely faceted scheme of classification

(71) Pre-Natal cataloguing was introduced by
(a) Dr Ranganathan (b) Library of Congress
(c) Dr P N Kaula (d) None of the above

(72) How many rules were in the catalogue code prepared by Charles C Jewett?
(a) 91 (b) 39
(c) 41 (d) 53

(73) What is Prussian Instruction?
(a) Rules of Management
(b) Rules of Cataloguing

(c) Rules of Computer

(d) Rules of Public library

(74) Identity from the following the name of the person who accepted corporate body as an author in cataloguing?

(a) C.A. Cutter

(b) Henry A sharp

(c) Dr. S.R. Ranganathan

(d) R. Watts.

(75) The electronic version of DDC 21(1996) named as

(a) Dewey for computer

(b) Dewey for window

(c) Dewey for electronic user

(d) DDC on screen

(76) RDA Toolkit is published by

(a) ALA, LA, SLA

(b) ALA, Library of congress, LA

(c) ALA, CLA, CILIP

(d) ALA, CLA, LA

(77) Influence of cinema on youth is an example of

(a) Inter Phase Relation

(b) Intra facet phase relation

(c) Inter away phase relation

(d) Intra Array relation

(78) An array is a group classes. It is

(a) Coordinate classes (b) Subordinate classes

(c) Chain of classes (d) Basic classes

(79) Common Isolate can be applicable to

(a) All subject (b) A few subject

(c) Most of the subject (d) None of the above

(80) MARC-1 was commenced in the year of

(a) 1966 (b) 1963
(c) 1974 (d) 1968

(81) Which form of ISBD emerged first
(a) ISBD (M) (b) ISBD (S)
(c) ISBD (CM) (d) ISBD (G)

(82) In UK MARC format 'Record Label' field is similar to USMARC
(a) Variable data field (b) Leader
(c) Directory (d) Control field

(83) International conference on cataloguing principle was held in
(a) 1971 (b) 1975
(c) 1961 (d) 1981

(84) Name the organisation who developed UNIMARC
(a) UNESCO (b) ASLIB
(c) ALA (d) IFLA

(85) In chain procedure false link associated with
(a) Indicator digit
(b) Class No.
(c) Concept suppose not searched by user
(d) Gap digit

(86) When was AACR-I prepared
(a) 1964 (b) 1963
(c) 1967 (d) 1968

(87) A person who uses the scheme of classification is called
(a) Documentalist (b) Classifier
(c) Classificationist (d) Librarian

(88) The array in which classes are arranged sub-ordinate in Idea Plane but appear to be co-ordinate in notational plane is called

(a) Interpolation
(b) Telescoped array
(c) Extrapolation of array
(d) Collateral Array

(89) Which agency has the authority to provide ISBN in India
(a) ILA
(b) NISCAIR
(c) RRRLF
(d) National Library Kolkata

(90) In India ISSN is assign by
(a) National Book Trust (b) DELNET
(c) NISSAT (d) NISCAIR

(91) Canon of Recall Value is enunciated in the year
(a) 1976 (b) 1969
(c) 1979 (d) 1975

(92) Which canon is called the master canon of cataloguing
(a) Canon of currency
(b) Canon of Recall value
(c) Canon of ascertainability
(d) Canon of sought heading

(93) Which canon emphasis for rendering information that found on the title page and its overflow pages
(a) Canon recall value
(b) Canon of prepotence
(c) Canon of consistency
(d) Canon of ascertain ability

(94) When two book Index entry are prepared for joint author reversing their name as heading element, following the

(a) Law of Impartiality
(b) Canon of Impartiality
(c) Laws of Interpretation
(d) Law of Parsimony

(95) The number of digit in ISSN are
(a) 12 (b) 08
(c) 13 (d) 10

(96) ISBN converted 10 digit to 13 digit in the year
(a) 2004 (b) 2007
(c) 2009 (d) 2005

(97) Colon classification IInd edition published in the year of
(a) 1937 (b) 1939
(c) 1959 (d) 1954

(98) Melvil Dewey was born on
(a) 10th December 1910 (b) 20 December 1941
(c) 10 December 1851 (d) 10 December 1892

(99) The famous book of classification prolegomena IIIrd edition published in
(a) 1937 (b) 1957
(c) 1967 (d) 1977

(100) In ISBN 10 digit,last digit is called
(a) Control digit (b) Title digit
(c) Publisher digit (d) Check digit

(101) International meeting of cataloguing experts held in
(a) London (b) Copenhagen
(c) New York (d) Netherlands

(102) What is the full name of CILIP
(a) Classification institute for Library & Information Practice

(b) Charted Institute for Library on Information publication

(c) Cataloguing institute for Library and Information profession

(d) Charted Institute for Library and Information professional

(103) MARC-21 is joint effort of

(a) ALA, LA, CLA (b) ALA, MARBI, LC

(c) LA, CLA, MARBI (d) MARBI, ASLIB, LA

(104) MeSH relate to

(a) Main English subject Heading

(b) Medical subject heading

(c) Medical short heading

(d) Medical subject Homepage

(105) Biochemistry is the result of

(a) Fission (b) Agglomeration

(c) Fusion (d) Lamination

(106) In AACR-2 in main entry if information is take from outside the source it is kept in

(a) Added entry (b) Curly Bracket

(c) Squire bracket (d) Parenthesis

(107) Match the following editions of DDC with their publishing year

(a) DDC 23rd (i) 1876

(b) DDC 19th (ii) 2011

(c) DDC 20th (iii) 1979

(d) DDC 1st (iv) 1989

	A	**B**	**C**	**D**
(a)	II	III	IV	I
(b)	III	IV	I	II
(c)	I	II	III	IV
(d)	IV	II	I	III

(108) Editor of DDC 23rd edition is

(a) William cook (b) Forest Press

(c) John Mitchell (d) William Fredrick

(109) ISBN introduced at International level in

(a) 1972 (b) 1974

(c) 1976 (d) 1978

(110) The first edition of CCF was published in the year

(a) 1974 (b) 1973

(c) 1984 (d) 1988

(111) CCF was developed by

(a) UNESCO (b) FID

(c) ICSO (d) IFLA

(112) Who is the author of the code "Rules for a printed dictionary catalog"

(a) Seymour Lubetzky (b) SR Ranganathon

(c) CA Cutter (d) A Panizzi

(113) Cutter's "Rules for a printed dictionary catalog" was first published in

(a) 1876 (b) 1891

(c) 1884 (d) 1899

(114) Bibliographic description requires tandardization to ensure

(a) Pure cataloguing (b) Recall

(c) Reference (d) Uniformity

(115) The Heading of corporate authorship in AACR-II is separated by

(a) Comma (b) Dot

(c) Semicolon (d) Colon

(116) The General International standard Bibliographic description is known as

(a) ISBD (M) (b) ISBD (GC)

(c) ISBD (G) (d) (G) ISBD

(117) In standard subdivision line number for Research in DDC is

(a) -06 (b) -072

(c) -05 (d) -03

(118) In UDC the symbol used to indicate relationships between two subjects is

(a) :colon (b) () Bracket

(c) + Plus (d) = Equal

(119) FRBR stands for

(a) Functional requirement for Bibliographic records

(b) Functional requirement for Bibliographic resources

(c) Fundamental requirement for Bibliography records

(d) Final requirement for Bibliographic resources

(120) Who has Introduced FRBR

(a) ICSSR (b) ASLIB

(c) OCLC (d) IFLA

(121) IFLA World library and information congress held in — during 17-23 August 2013

(a) Madrid (b) Singapore

(c) London (d) New Jersey

(122) Chicago manual of style related to

(a) Cataloguing (b) Computer

(c) Classification (d) Management

(123) Dissection implies

(a) Forming co-ordinate classes

(b) Forming sub-ordinate classes

(c) Forming phase relation

(d) Forming classes at both level chain as well as array

(124) Denudation implies

(a) Forming Classes at sub ordinate level

(b) Forming classes at co-ordinate

(c) Forming lower classes

(d) Forming partial comprehension

(125) In AACR2 rendering the information about a conference as author year and place of conference is written

(a) Square bracket

(b) Within 2 separate circular bracket

(c) Within one circular bracket with colon

(d) Within one square bracket without colon

(126) Which one is not a canon

(a) Canon of comprehensiveness

(b) Canon of context

(c) Canon of Individualization

(d) Canon of currency

(127) The principle of Local variation is mainly applicable in

(a) Cataloguing (b) Reference service

(c) Circulation (d) Acquisition

(128) The term "literary Warrant" was introduced by

(a) E J Coats (b) E Wyndham Hulme

(c) Shepherd (d) Thomas Richard

(129) In Classification canon of currency found at

(a) Verbal Plane

(b) National Plane

(c) Idea Plane

(d) Laws of Library Science

(130) The array in which classes are sub-ordinate in Idea Plane but appear to be co-ordinate in national plane is known by

(a) Interpolation in Array
(b) Telescoping Array
(c) Extrapolation in Array
(d) None of the above

ANSWERS

(1) b	(2) b	(3) a	(4) b
(5) d	(6) b	(7) c	(8) c
(9) a	(10) c	(11) b	(12) d
(13) b	(14) c	(15) d	(16) c
(17) c	(18) b	(19) d	(20) b
(21) c	(22) d	(23) a	(24) c
(25) b	(26) b	(27) a	(28) d
(29) b	(30) b	(31) a	(32) b
(33) a	(34) a	(35) c	(36) a
(37) a	(38) c	(39) c	(40) a
(41) d	(42) b	(43) c	(44) c
(45) c	(46) d	(47) c	(48) d
(49) b	(50) b	(51) a	(52) b
(53) d	(54) c	(55) b	(56) b
(57) c	(58) b	(59) c	(60) d
(61) c	(62) a	(63) a	(64) b
(65) a	(66) b	(67) b	(68) c
(69) c	(70) a	(71) a	(72) b
(73) b	(74) a	(75) b	(76) c
(77) a	(78) a	(79) c	(80) a
(81) a	(82) b	(83) c	(84) d
(85) a	(86) c	(87) b	(88) b
(89) c	(90) d	(91) b	(92) b
(93) d	(94) a	(95) b	(96) b
(97) b	(98) c	(99) c	(100) d
(101) b	(102) d	(103) b	(104) b
(105) c	(106) c	(107) a	(108) c
(109) a	(110) c	(111) d	(112) c
(113) a	(114) d	(115) b	(116) c
(117) b	(118) a	(119) a	(120) d
(121) b	(122) a	(123) a	(124) a
(125) c	(126) a	(127) a	(128) b
(129) a	(130) b		

2
Information Technology and Library Automation

(1) First mechanical adding machine is devised by

(a) Dr. Smith (b) J.H. Quinn

(c) Baron Gotti Fried (d) Blaise Pascal

(2) It was devised in the year of

(a) 1972 (b) 1642

(c) 1782 (d) 1884

(3) Who has devised the concept of punched cards as input device

(a) Robert Dennard (b) William Von

(c) Herman Hollerith (d) Robert Peterson

(4) Charles Babbage introduced ——— in 1822

(a) Search engine (b) Difference Engine

(c) Steam engine (d) Differ Analytical engine

(5) The mark I Computer designed by

(a) A. Josef (b) A Aiken with IBM

(c) Dr. John (d) None of these

(6) The ENIAC refers to

(a) Electronic Numerical Integrator and calculator
(b) Electronic Number Input and computer
(c) Electric Numerical Integrator and calculator
(d) Electric Numbering Intelligent computer

(7) EDVAC computer was devised by
(a) Thomas Colmar
(b) Dr. John von Neumann
(c) John Napier
(d) Mill Gates

(8) UNIVAC I (1951) refers to
(a) Universe Access computer
(b) Universal Automatic computer
(c) Universal Auto calculator
(d) United Automatic computer

(9) Use of vacuum tubes is a feature of-
(a) Second generation computer
(b) Forth generation computer
(c) First generation computer
(d) None of these

(10) Third Generation computer with IC introduced between
(a) 1960-1975 (b) 1962-1972
(c) 1964-1975 (d) 1965-1975

(11) FORTRAN, COBOL are the
(a) Second generation computer languages
(b) Third generation computer language
(c) Fourth generation computer languages
(d) None of these

(12) PCs are the boon of
(a) Fourth generation computer
(b) Third generation computer

(c) Second generation computer

(d) None of the above

(13) Which features have Fourth generation computers

(i) Networking (ii) Artificial Intelligent

(iii) GUI (iv) CD-ROM

(a) Only I and IV (b) Only I and III

(c) Only II and III (d) Only II and IV

(14) In Hexadecimal number system 10 will be written as

(a) B (b) C

(c) 0 (d) A

(15) Hexadecimal number system has a base of

(a) 16 numbers (b) 15 numbers

(c) 8 numbers (d) 2 numbers

(16) Octal no system has a base of 8 that is

(a) 1 – 8 (b) 0 – 7

(c) 0 – 8 (d) 1 – 7

(17) BCD code stand for

(a) Binary computer digit

(b) Bit computer decimal

(c) Binary coded decimal

(d) Binary coded digit

(18) EBC DIC is a

(a) 16 bit code (b) 8 bit code

(c) 6 bit code (d) 0 bit code

(19) Unicode supports

(a) Only English language

(b) Only French Language

(c) Multi Lingual work

(d) None of the above

(20) A new CPU manufactured, it has all the instruction of its predecessor. This strategy is known as

(a) CPU +

(b) CPU ++

(c) Backward compatibility

(d) Forward compatibility

(21) Cache memory works

(a) In main memory

(b) CPU

(c) Between CPU and Main Memory

(d) In secondary memory & main memory

(22) When power off, the primary storage loses data this is a type of

(a) Volatile memory (b) Non-volatile memory

(c) Secondary memory (d) Cache memory

(23) A magnetic disk contains

(a) Only circles (b) Only sectors

(c) Circles and tracks (d) Tracks and sectors

(24) Digital video disk is a/an

(a) Magnetic disk (b) Optical disk

(c) PD (d) Magnetic tape device

(25) Memory card is also known as

(a) Smart card

(b) Flash drive

(c) Secure digital/multimedia card

(d) Secure device/multimedia card

(26) MICR technology is used commonly in

(a) Schools (b) Markets

(c) Banks (d) Malls

(27) The work of system software is

(i) To support the application software

(ii) To control operation of peripheral devices

(iii) To control human ware

(iv) Provide current to the system

(a) Only I and II (b) Only I and III

(c) Only III and IV (d) Only I

(28) Database software is an

(a) System software

(b) Application software

(c) Both A and B

(d) Program written in human language

(29) Identify from the following which symbols are applied in flow chart

(i) Terminal ⬭ (ii) Processing ▭

(iii) Decision ◇ (iv) Triangle △

(a) I, II IV (b) I II III

(c) I and II only (d) I and III only

(30) Machine language is a combination of

(a) 0 and 1

(b) Low level language & high level language

(c) Interpreter & compiler

(d) None of the above

(31) Assembler is used to convert —— in to machine language

(a) High level language (b) Low level language

(c) Assembly language (d) Both B + C

(32) High level language are

(a) Machine dependent (b) Machine Independent

(c) Both a + b (d) None of the above

(33) Compiler is used to translate

(a) High level language into machine language

(b) Machine language into high level language

(c) Assembly language
(d) Pseudo language

(34) FORTRAN, a high level language stands for
(a) Foreign Translator
(b) Formula Translation
(c) Formula Transmission
(d) Formula Technique

(35) BASIC stands for
(a) Beginners at symbolic Instruction code
(b) Beginners all systematic instruction code
(c) Beginners all purpose symbolic instruction code
(d) Begin at software instruction & command

(36) In multiprogramming we use
(a) Uniprocessor
(b) More than one language
(c) More than one machine
(d) None of the above

(37) In multiprocessing processes are run on
(a) Single processor or uniprocessor
(b) Multiple processors
(c) More than one computer
(d) Processes running on LAN

(38) Identify multiuser operating systems
(i) MS-DOS (ii) UNIX
(iii) Windows NT (iv) Window XP
(a) Only I (b) Only I and II
(c) Only II and III (d) Only IV

(39) In file access method if we find content in a sequence it is called
(a) Random access
(b) Sequential access

(c) Access from back information
(d) Access from any location

(40) In random file access system access for a particular record can be done
(a) Sequentially (b) Randomly
(c) A+B (d) None of the above

(41) The example of random access file are
(i) Magnetic tape (ii) Optical disk
(iii) Magnetic disk (iv) Floppy
(a) Only I (b) II and III
(c) Only IV (d) II only

(42) Which operating system has differentiation in lower case and upper case letter in file naming
(i) UNIX (ii) MS-DOS
(iii) I and II (iv) None of the above
(a) Only I (b) Only III
(c) IV (d) I

(43) If you want to prevent unauthorized access to your file or information which mechanism would you apply
(a) Antivirus (b) Data backup
(c) Cryptography (d) None of the above

(44) MS-EXCEL is a
(a) Word processing package
(b) Graphics package
(c) Spreadsheet package
(d) Personal assistance package

(45) Rows and columns are the essential elements of
(a) Network data base
(b) Hierarchical database
(c) Relational database
(d) Object oriented database

(46) Identify the main components of DBMS.

(i) Data Definition Language

(ii) Data manipulation language

(iii) Data exporting language

(iv) Query language

(a) I, II, IV (b) I, II, III

(c) II, III, IV (d) IV and I

(47) Identify from the following which is not an element of communication system

(a) Sender (b) Receiver

(c) Ambassador (d) Medium

(48) In this mode of data transmission data flow in both direction simultaneously.

(a) Simplex mode (b) Half duplex mode

(c) Full duplex mode (d) None of the above

(49) The way in which the network's nodes are linked together is called

(a) Strategy

(b) Mode of data communication

(c) Topology

(d) Analog

(50) A type of topology that contains multiple nodes connected to a host node

(a) Ring topology (b) Star topology

(c) Bus topology (d) None of these

(51) It is a set of formal operating rules, procedure or conventions that govern a given process. It is called

(a) Proceed (b) Solution

(c) Protocol (d) Procedure

(52) How many layers have an OSI model ?

(a) 7 (b) 6

(c) 5 (d) 4

(53) Which protocol enables user to move a file from one computer to another on the internet?

(a) Telnet
(b) Router
(c) FTP
(d) Data routing protocol

(54) Ram sends a file to his friend on computer by using internet. This process is called

(a) Uploading
(b) Downloading
(c) Uploading/Downloading
(d) Hyperlink

(55) When more than one medium is used to represent the information it is called

(a) Unimediam presentation
(b) Multimedium presentation
(c) Oral presentation
(d) Written presentation

(56) Hypermedia contains information in it about

(a) Only text
(b) Only graphics
(c) Text, sound and graphics
(d) Vocabulary

(57) Which is not a web browser

(a) Yahoo
(b) Kindle
(c) Hotpot
(d) Info seek

(58) The term Hypertext was coined by

(a) E Garfield
(b) G. William
(c) Ted Nelson
(d) Robert

(59) Identify from the following which is a system software

(a) World star
(b) MS-Office
(c) Windows 98
(d) Kundli pro

(60) Apache is a

(a) Web sever (b) Search engine

(c) Web browser (d) None of the above

(61) Who coined the word Web 2.0

(a) A Thomas (b) Ted Nelson

(c) Davis Moore (d) Casey

(62) Kindle is a device used

(a) For theses preservation

(b) For reading Braille book

(c) For reading E-book

(d) For purchasing gift online

(63) Which of the following is not a microform

(a) Microfilm (b) Microfiche

(c) Micro computer (d) Catalogue cabinet

(64) Arrange the following storage devices according to their increasing capacity

(i) Magnetic tape (ii) CD-ROM

(iii) Floppy (iv) Magnetic disk

(a) III, I, II, IV (b) I, II, III, IV

(c) IV, III, I, II (d) III, IV, I, II

(65) In computer terminology an error in a program is known as

(a) BUS (b) Error

(c) Virus (d) BUG.

(66) Who has invented microchip ?

(a) IBM (b) INTEL

(c) Infosys (d) BARC

(67) The first electronic computer called ABC was devised by

(a) Howard Read

(b) J P Eckert

(c) JV Aton soft and C Berry

(d) Madam Ada

(68) Which of the following is not a programming language

(a) FORTRAN (b) COBOL

(c) C++ (d) ASCII

(69) Match the following

(A) Key board (i) Keeping records

(B) Control unit (ii) Output device

(C) Visual display unit (iii) Common Input devices

(D) DBMS (iv) Relate to CPU

	A	B	C	D
(a)	I,	II,	III,	IV
(b)	III,	IV,	II,	I
(c)	IV,	I,	III,	II
(d)	II,	I,	III,	IV

(70) Tree topology is the extended form of

(a) Bus topology (b) Ring topology

(c) Star topology (d) Hybrid topology

(71) Information technology Act passed in the year

(a) 1998 (b) 2000

(c) 2001 (d) 2002

(72) Expert system of knowledge is the boon of

(a) Artificial intelligence (b) Relational database

(c) Web 2.0 (d) None of the above

(73) Which is not a component of expert system

(a) Knowledge base (b) DBMS

(c) Inference engine (d) User interface

(74) Digital library is a library where

(a) Housekeeping operation are computerized

(b) Library contains books and audio-visual resource

(c) Content of the document are digitized

(d) Content of the thesaurus are digitized

(75) Which service is providing link to UGC Infonet 2.0 program

(a) BSNL (b) ERNET

(c) NIC (d) VSNL

(76) Institutional Repository are the digitized format of

(a) All academic information of members of Institution

(b) All student's information of university

(c) All Institution of a subject

(d) Content created by member of an institution

(77) First computerized Journal is

(a) Index medicus

(b) Journal of Biochemistry

(c) Journal of science

(d) Chemical titles

(78) Shodhganga is a

(a) International Research Centre

(b) Name of digital library

(c) Repository of Indian thesis

(d) Cataloguing

(79) What is Joomla ?

(a) A computerized consortia service

(b) Name of digital library

(c) A library portal

(d) Open source content management system

(80) Computer is not called as one of the following

(a) Data processor (b) Micro computer

(c) Artificial Intelligence (d) Data interpreter

(81) Natural language refers to

(a) Programming language

(b) Assembly language

(c) Machine language

(d) Spoken language

(82) Match the following library software with their originator

(A) Libsis	(i) Delnet
(B) CDS/ISIS	(ii) Libsis corporation
(C) Sanjay	(iii) UNESCO
(D) Del-plus	(iv) DESIDOC

	A	B	C	D
(a)	II,	I,	III,	IV
(b)	II,	III,	I,	IV
(c)	II,	III,	IV,	I
(d)	IV,	III,	I,	II

(83) The First online database introduced is

(a) OCLC (b) DIALOG

(c) BRS (d) RELIN

(84) What is Del-plus

(a) A software for library management

(b) A computer language

(c) Digital library

(d) Delhi project

(85) It is the short name of modulation and demodulation

(a) Modules of software

(b) Modem

(c) Memory

(d) Medium of communication

(86) In packet switching every packet has the information equal to

(a) 100 bit

(b) Approximately 1000 bit

(c) Approximately 10000 bit

(d) None of the above

(87) LAN supported version of CDS/ISIS is

(a) Version 1.0 (b) Version 2.0

(c) Version 3.0 (d) Windows version 1.0

(88) Pick out the step that is not associated with CDS/ ISIS database preparation

(a) FDT (b) Data Worksheet

(c) Record (d) Reference Service

(89) Which is not a computer language

(a) Fortran (b) C++

(c) World cat (d) C#

(90) Blog is also called

(a) Catalog (b) Weblog

(c) Web-site (d) Blogger

(91) Who is the devcloper of "software for university library"

(a) INFLIBNET (b) UGC-INFONET

(c) DESIDOC (d) NISCAIR

(92) 1974-1985 is the time of

(a) First generation computer

(b) Second generation computer

(c) Third generation computer

(d) Fourth generation computer

(93) A set of computer program is known as

(a) Hardware (b) Human ware

(c) Firmware (d) Software

(94) It is a way to provide personal & social information and entries are arranged reverse chronologically. What is it?

(a) Communication on telephone
(b) Blog
(c) Open source software
(d) Face book

(95) 'Karuna' is an example of

(a) Human feeling
(b) Open source software
(c) Digital library of Ayurveda
(d) Indian version of MARC-21

(96) EMBASE is a database relate to the field of

(a) Library science
(b) Chemistry
(c) Medicine
(d) Electronic management

(97) CERN relate to

(a) FA Lancaster (b) VC Bickery
(c) K C Harrison (d) Tim Berner Lee

(98) Who provides ISP to the government department in India

(a) Infosys (b) VSNL
(c) NIC (d) INDONET

(99) Web crawler is the another name of

(a) Web site (b) Internet explorer
(c) Web portal (d) Search engine

(100) RFID has 3 components. These are

(a) Antenna, transceiver, transponder
(b) Antenna, transmission language
(c) Language, transponder, antenna
(d) Antenna, tags, instrument

(101) What is PHP
- (a) Server side scripting language
- (b) Highlevel Advance language
- (c) Protocal
- (d) Advance HTML

(102) In cloud computing
- (a) User terminal have all necessary software
- (b) User terminal have OS and web browser only
- (c) User terminal has only operating software
- (d) User terminal has only networking and C# language

(103) ASCII stands for
- (a) American standard code for international information
- (b) American subject code for information index
- (c) American standard code for information introduction
- (d) American standard code for information interchange

(104) IBM stands for
- (a) International business machine
- (b) Information bibliography machine
- (c) International Burean of Management
- (d) None of these

(105) SLIM 21 is a
- (a) Directoring of 21 century libraries
- (b) Database of library of congress
- (c) Software for library management
- (d) Open source software

(106) DAISY is an Information system
- (a) For doctors
- (b) For blind
- (c) For librarian
- (d) For academics

(107) E-print open source software is developed by

(a) University of California

(b) University of Chicago

(c) London University

(d) University of Southampton

(108) In computer networking OSI stands for

(a) Open space information

(b) Open software intergradations

(c) Open system interconnection

(d) Open source information

(109) The OSI model consists

(a) Five layers (b) Seven layers

(c) Eight layers (d) Two layers

(110) W3C stands for

(a) World wide classification

(b) World wide web content

(c) World wide web consortia

(d) World wide web cataloguing

(111) Virus is a software which can

(a) Manipulate data (b) Replicate itself

(c) Damage computer (d) All the above

(112) Which one of the protocol is used in file transfer over internet

(a) TCP/IP (b) SMTP

(c) FTP (d) PUP

(113) Web portal is also known as

(a) Common portal (b) Public portal

(c) Population portal (d) Gateway

(114) Internet librarian conference was held during 28-30 october 2013 at

(a) New Jersy (b) California

(c) New York (d) Bostan

(115) Mooc refers to

(a) Mass communication open on line

(b) Massive open online cources

(c) Medical open online cources

(d) MIT online open cataloguing

(116) Who has designed and developed Info-port

(a) UGC-CSIR (b) INFLIBNET

(c) CSIR network (d) NISSAT

(117) Netscape means

(a) Institute of Information

(b) Browser

(c) Application software

(d) Language

(118) The term 'blog' shortest version of 'Weblog' is given by

(a) Willion Fredrick (b) V.K. naidu

(c) Peter merholz (d) Peter cook

(119) Name the first commercial on line database

(a) RELIN (b) BRS

(c) DIALOG (d) MEDLARS

(120) The second generation of World wide web technology is known as

(a) Web 2.0 (b) World wide web II

(c) WWW2 (d) None of the above

(121) What is library 2.0

(a) Type of library

(b) Second generation of public library

(c) Involves user participation in technological and content upgradation

(d) Involves only librarian of present era

(122) Who coined the word library 2.0

(a) Ellussa Kroski (b) John Mussey
(c) Michael casey (d) WC William

(123) RSS is a

(a) Open source catalog
(b) Web feed format
(c) Ready search service
(d) A software of facebook

(124) Really simple syndication (RSS) is also known by another name, that is

(a) Rich simple syntex (b) Really simple source
(c) Rich site summary (d) Really site summary

(125) OSS is provided with

(a) Object code
(b) Only source code
(c) Source code with licence to use it freely
(d) None of the above

(126) EAN-13 barcode is now known as

(a) International Access number
(b) International Account Number
(c) International Article number
(d) Earn Article number

(127) International Article number previously known as

(a) European Access number
(b) European Article number
(c) European Access notation
(d) Euro Account Number

(128) eGyankosh is a national digital repository, contains digital resources

(a) Developed by Research Institution
(b) Developed by open and distance learning Institution

(c) Developed by public library

(d) Developed by Academic library

(129) FORSA consortia for resource sharing is related to the field of

(a) Science and Technology

(b) Medicine

(c) Astronomy and Astrophysis

(d) Food & Agriculture

(130) Digital library of library & Information science related to Indian librarianship is developed by

(a) NISCAIR (b) DELNET

(c) ILA (d) DRTC

(131) Wiki pedians are the persons

(a) Who use Wikipedia

(b) Who access & retrieve content of wikipedia

(c) Who write and edit content of wikipedia

(d) Who are in permanent editorial board of wikipedia

(132) Which field from the following WINISIS does not have

(a) FDT (b) Data entry worksheet

(c) Directory (d) PFT

(133) Google library project is an online searching of

(a) Libraries of the world

(b) Books

(c) Library of google tools

(d) Serials

(134) Open Archives Initiatives consists standard for

(a) Library building (b) Library teaching

(c) Interoperability (d) OSI

(135) "National RFID Program" Project was initiated in

(a) April 2006 (b) April 2005

(c) April 2007 (d) April 2013

(136) The inverted file also known as

(a) Directory (b) Sequential file

(c) Indexes (d) Record

(137) Interacting IR system when user cannot express his requirement clearly. It is called

(a) Nil Knowledge

(b) Anomalous state of knowledge

(c) Knowledge barrier

(d) Lack of knowledge

(138) CDS/ISIS 2.0 is designed using the language

(a) C++ (b) C

(c) Pascal (d) Lisp

(139) IIT Delhi metadata Harvesting service is known as

(a) Cultivation (b) SEED

(c) HARVEST (d) CAPTURE

(140) Match following software of library Management with their development

(a) SOUL (i) Infosys, Pune

(b) ALICE (ii) Softlink Asia, New Delhi

(c) DEL-Windows (iii) INFLIBNET

(d) TLMS (iv) DELNET, New Delhi

	A	B	C	D
(a)	I	II	III	IV
(b)	III	II	IV	I
(c)	II	I	IV	III
(d)	I	IV	III	II

(141) Who is the distributer of CDS/ISIS in India

(a) NISCAIR (b) NIC

(c) NISSAT (d) DELNET

(142) Identity the software considered as first open source software

(a) Green stone (b) E-print

(c) KOHA (d) DSpace'

(143) Which one search engine is oldest search engine

(a) AltaVista (b) Yahoo

(c) Google (d) Northern light

(144) PHP stands for

(a) Protocol of home page

(b) Hypertext pre processor

(c) Personal hyper page

(d) Personal hidden page

(145) What is PHP?

(a) Server side scripting language

(b) High level advance language

(c) Protocol

(d) Advance HTML

(146) TCP/IP Architecture consist

(a) Five layers (b) Seven layers

(c) Six layers (d) Two layers

(147) Which layer is responsible to convert the data into a stream of bits

(a) Physical layer (b) Network layer

(c) Data link layer (d) Application layer

(148) What is Novell Netware

(a) A type of network

(b) First network operating system

(c) Type of library

(d) Dictionery of computer terms

(149) In entity relationship model teacher and students have a relation, that is

(a) One to one relationship

(b) One to many relationship

(c) Many to many

(d) None of these

(150) Identify from the following which is not the major component of E-R model

(a) Entity (b) Attributes

(c) Pascal language (d) Relationship

(151) DBMS consists data dictionary its work is

(a) To provide meaning of different word of user

(b) To have information about data element in database

(c) To put query statement

(d) In deny access of unauthorized person

(152) Data dictionary is also known as

(a) Metadata (b) Source data

(c) Numerical data (d) Alphabetical dictionary

(153) Mail merge is found in this menu

(a) Edit menu (b) Table menu

(c) View menu (d) Tool menu

(154) MS-Excel worksheet contains

(a) 66,256 rows and 256 columns

(b) 65,536 rows 256 columns

(c) 65,536 rows and 252 columns

(d) 65,536 rows and 200 columns

(155) In MS-Excel the cell with highlighted boundary is called

(a) Current cell (b) Active cell

(c) Working cell (d) Virtual cell

(156) SAMEER stands for

(a) society for magnetic Engineering and research

(b) System for applied engineers

(c) Society for microwave engineers

(d) Society for applied microwave electronic engineering & research

(157) Library 2.013 Virtual conference was held on 18-19 October 2013 at USA hosted by

(a) San Jone state university

(b) OCLC

(c) Columbia University

(d) Ohio University

(158) What is webinars

(a) New technology of web

(b) Dictionary of websites

(c) Conference through web

(d) A journal of Website technology

(159) Relate the following

(A)	Greenstone	(i)	HP and MIT libraries
(B)	E-print	(ii)	Waikato New-Zealand
(C)	Dspace	(iii)	University of south Hampton
(D)	Fedora	(iv)	Cornell University

	A	B	C	D
(a)	I	II	III	IV
(b)	II	III	IV	I
(c)	II	III	I	IV
(d)	IV	I	III	II

(160) SCONUL stands for

(a) Set support colleges national university libraries

(b) Society of college, nation university libraries

(c) Society for Cultural national libraries

(d) None of the above

(161) SCONUL (US) Supported

(a) Academic libraries (b) Special libraries

(c) National Libraries (d) Public libraries

(162) ACRL refers to

(a) Association of complete research libraries

(b) Association of chemistry Research library

(c) Association of college and research libraries (USA)

(d) Advancement in college and research libraries

(163) ACRL is a division of

(a) NML (b) ALA

(c) SLA (d) OCLC

(164) SLIS of San José state university of USA remain in limelight during 18-19 October 2013 for which purpose

(a) National conference

(b) Online world wide virtual conference

(c) Library science in teaching

(d) Social science conference

(165) Info Port is a

(a) Institute of information

(b) Gateway of Indian Electronic resources

(c) Electronic content Analysis centre

(d) Information portable to internet

(166) Who has designed and developed Info-port

(a) UGC-CSIR (b) INFLIBNET

(c) DELNET (d) NIC

(167) National informatics centre in India established in

(a) 1975 (b) 1988

(c) 1977 (d) 1951

(168) INFLIBNET emerged in

(a) 1987 (b) 1988

(c) 1990 (d) 1997

(169) Identify from the following which organisation in library science first, used computer

(a) Indian statistical institute

(b) NISCAIR

(c) National library

(d) DRTC

(170) SAMEER established in India at Mumbai in

(a) 1980 (b) 1984

(c) 1988 (d) 1990

(171) SIS refers to

(a) Society for interception security

(b) Society for information science

(c) Society for information security

(d) Society for information system

(172) JSIR refers to

(a) Journal System information retrieval

(b) Journal of Scientific and industrial research

(c) Science in research network

(d) None of the above

(173) SIRNET is prepared by

(a) NIC (b) CMC

(c) Bits Pilani (d) NISCAIR

(174) Dspace open source software is not using by this institute

(a) INFLIBNET

(b) National institute of oceanography

(c) Aryabhatta research institute of observational science

(d) CSJM university

(175) WOS refers to

(a) Word of science (b) Work of science

(c) Web of science (d) World of science

(176) What is Z39.50

(a) Size of book racks

(b) Size of functional libraries

(c) Communication protocol

(d) Name of topology

(177) Z39.50 protocol's standard is maintained by

(a) Delnet (b) OCLC

(c) CILIF (d) Library of congress

(178) What is webfeed

(a) Creation of website

(b) Putting information in web architecture

(c) Provide current updates created in website to end user

(d) Technological error

(179) RSS and ATOM are

(a) Standard of web feed

(b) New Websites

(c) Digital liberties of world

(d) None of the above

(180) Who is the owner of Internet

(a) American mathematical society

(b) Department of science and technology govt of India

(c) British standard institute

(d) None of the above

(181) NACLIN is sponsored by

(a) INFLIBNET (b) CALIBNET

(c) NIC NET (d) DELNET

(182) The correct chronological order of following libraries software is

(a) CDS/ISIS, SOUL, Green stone, D-Space

(b) D-space, SOUL, CDS/ISIS, Green stone
(c) Green stone, CDS/ISIS, D space, SOUL
(d) SOUL, D-space, Green stone, CDS/ISIS

(183) Arrange the following in chronological order according to their origin

(i) Unix (ii) MS Dos
(iii) Linux (iv) Windows NT

(a)	IV	II	I	III
(b)	II	I	IV	III
(c)	II	I	III	IV
(d)	I	II	III	IV

(184) Which font would you choose for Hindi Typing

(a) New roman Font (b) Kurtidev font
(c) Kunti Font (d) Kamayani font

(185) What is BUBL link

(a) British library link
(b) Catalog of Internet resources
(c) Institution repository
(d) INDEST Consortia link

(186) Roger K. Summit was the director of

(a) DIALOG (b) SDC
(c) MEDLARS (d) RR Bowker

(187) INDEST consortium was set-up in

(a) 2000 (b) 2003
(c) 2006 (d) 2010

(188) INDEST consortium was renamed as INDEST-AICTE

(a) 2003 (b) 2004
(c) 2002 (d) 2005

(189) Who is now the electronic publisher of Dialog

(a) R.R. Bowker (b) Thomson Reuters
(c) Pro Quest (d) H.W. Wilson

(190) It is largest on line public access catalog

(a) Catalog one line (b) World cat

(c) World catalog (d) All Catalog

(191) Which institute has started UDC online

(a) FID (b) UDCC

(c) OCLC (d) Library of congress

ANSWERS

(1) d	(2) b	(3) d	(4) b
(5) b	(6) c	(7) b	(8) b
(9) c	(10) c	(11) a	(12) a
(13) b	(14) d	(15) a	(16) b
(17) c	(18) b	(19) c	(20) c
(21) b	(22) a	(23) c	(24) b
(25) c	(26) c	(27) a	(28) b
(29) b	(30) a	(31) c	(32) b
(33) a	(34) b	(35) c	(36) a
(37) b	(38) c	(39) b	(40) b
(41) b	(42) a	(43) c	(44) c
(45) c	(46) a	(47) c	(48) c
(49) c	(50) b	(51) c	(52) a
(53) c	(54) a	(55) b	(56) c
(57) b	(58) c	(59) c	(60) a
(61) d	(62) c	(63) d	(64) a
(65) d	(66) b	(67) c	(68) d
(69) b	(70) a	(71) b	(72) a
(73) b	(74) c	(75) a	(76) d
(77) d	(78) c	(79) d	(80) d
(81) d	(82) c	(83) b	(84) a
(85) b	(86) b	(87) c	(88) d
(89) c	(90) b	(91) a	(92) d
(93) d	(94) b	(95) b	(96) c
(97) d	(98) c	(99) d	(100) a
(101) a	(102) b	(103) d	(104) a
(105) c	(106) b	(107) d	(108) b
(109) b	(110) c	(111) d	(112) c
(113) b	(114) b	(115) b	(116) b

(117) b	(118) c	(119) c	(120) a
(121) c	(122) c	(123) b	(124) c
(125) c	(126) c	(127) b	(128) b
(129) c	(130) d	(131) c	(132) c
(133) b	(134) c	(135) c	(136) c
(137) b	(138) c	(139) b	(140) b
(141) c	(142) c	(143) b	(144) b
(145) a	(146) a	(147) a	(148) b
(149) b	(150) c	(151) b	(152) a
(153) d	(154) b	(155) b	(156) d
(157) a	(158) c	(159) c	(160) b
(161) a	(162) c	(163) b	(164) b
(165) b	(166) b	(167) a	(168) b
(169) a	(170) b	(171) b	(172) c
(173) d	(174) d	(175) c	(176) c
(177) d	(178) c	(179) a	(180) d
(181) d	(182) a	(183) c	(184) b
(185) b	(186) a	(187) b	(188) d
(189) c	(190) b	(191) b	

3
Reference Services

(1) Treatment, format, scope are the criteria related to
  (a) Classification of documents
  (b) Evaluation of reference sources
  (c) Digitations of books
  (d) Cataloguing of non-book material

(2) It is world's largest Abstracting service
  (a) Chemical Abstract (b) Biological Abstract
  (c) LISA (d) Physics Abstract

(3) American Chemical Society publishing this Abstract periodical since 1907
  (a) Psychological Abstract
  (b) Chemical Abstract
  (c) BIOSIS
  (d) Physics Abstract

(4) Which Index is called News Paper Index
  (a) Current content
  (b) Social science Index
  (c) Indian Press Index
  (d) Cataloguing of non-book material

(5) Facts on file "current reference source" Publish from

(a) New Delhi (b) London

(c) New York (d) Tokyo

(6) Asian Recorder is a

(a) Weekly Index (b) Monthly Index

(c) Bimonthly Index (d) None of the Above

(7) Who is the publisher of current content Indexing service

(a) Wilson

(b) Institute for scientific information

(c) Indian documentation centre

(d) R.R. Bowker

(8) 'Bibliography' word has been derived from

(a) Greek word (b) Latin word

(c) German word (d) French word

(9) What is the frequency of INB after 1963 ?

(a) Monthly (b) Weekly

(c) Quarterly (d) Yearly

(10) Who is the publisher of INB?

(a) Central Reference Library of NL

(b) NISCAIR

(c) DRTC

(d) Ministry of Information

(11) INB remain suspended between

(a) 1960-63 (b) 1964-65

(c) 1967-71 (d) 1980-81

(12) British National Bibliography has been publishing since

(a) 1950 (b) 1948

(c) 1951 (d) 1957

(13) LISA is published by

(a) British Library
(b) Library Association UK
(c) American Library Association
(d) H W Wilson London

(14) Physics Abstract is published by
(a) Institute of Computer Engineers
(b) Institute of Electrical Engineers
(c) Institute for scientific information
(d) Institute for science Today

(15) Who is the first Librarian of National Library of Calcutta
(a) Dr. S.R. Ranganathan
(b) B.S. Keshwan
(c) C. Majumdar
(d) G. Bhattacharya

(16) Who is the publisher of ISA
(a) NISCAIR
(b) NISSAT
(c) Institute for science Information
(d) Indian documentation service

(17) Encyclopedia Britannica Published its first edition in between of
(a) 1769-71 (b) 1768-71
(c) 1770-73 (d) 1770-74

(18) This part of Britannica encyclopedia provide outline of any field of knowledge
(a) Propaedia (b) Micropaedia
(c) Macropaedia (d) None of the above

(19) Mc-Grow. Hill Encyclopedia of science and Technology first published in
(a) 1945 (b) 1948
(c) 1958 (d) 1960

(20) Who is the publisher of International Encyclopaedia of social science

(a) R.R. Bowker

(b) H.W. Wilson

(c) MacMillan, Crowell, Collier

(d) Institute for social science

(21) Name the publication place of encyclopedia of library and information science

(a) London (b) New York

(c) Chicago (d) New Jersey

(22) Statesman's year book has been publishing since

(a) 1864 (b) 1464

(c) 1960 (d) 1850

(23) If you want to know about the life of USA president Barak Obama which source would you consult

(a) Bibliography

(b) Guide to Literature

(c) Biographical dictionary

(d) Almanac

(24) World of Learning is a

(a) Bibliography (b) Dictionary

(c) Year Book (d) Directory

(25) Patents are regarded as

(a) Primary sources (b) Secondary sources

(c) Tertiary sources (d) Auxiliary sources

(26) Index Medicus is produced by

(a) Library Association

(b) Medical Association of London

(c) MEDLARS

(d) Doctors of Medical Library

(27) The source for finding astronomical information is

(a) Almanac (b) Encyclopedia
(c) Year Book (d) Directory

(28) Lexicography is the art and science of preparing
(a) Encyclopedia
(b) Directories
(c) Biographical dictionary
(d) Dictionaries

(29) Method of assessing information need of user is known as
(a) Education of user (b) User studies
(c) User orientation (d) Information to user

(30) India: a reference annual is regarded as
(a) Year book (b) Almanac
(c) Guide Book (d) Bibliography

(31) Directing the user to the centers from where he/she can get his/her information is known as
(a) Reference Service (b) Referral service
(c) Information science (d) SDI

(32) For selection of periodicals the appropriate source is
(a) Dictionary
(b) Year book
(c) Ulrich periodical directory
(d) World of Learning

(33) To know the name and address of world's learned societies and organizations, the appropriate source will be
(a) World of Learning
(b) University hand book
(c) Statesmen year book
(d) Indian: a reference annual

(34) The publisher of encyclopedia Americana is

(a) Dekker (b) Grolier

(c) Colliers (d) Mc-Grow-Hill

(35) Which Encyclopaedia has its expansion in 30 volumes

(a) Encyclopaedia Britannica

(b) Encyclopaedia Americana

(c) International Encyclopaedia of social sciences

(d) Encyclopaedia of Religion and Ethics

(36) Compiler of NUCSSI.

(a) NISCAIR (b) SSDC

(c) ICSSR (d) DRTC

(37) Index India's publication place is

(a) New Delhi (b) Bangalore

(c) Jaipur (d) Hyderabad

(38) The publication place of Whitaker's Almanac is

(a) New York (b) London

(c) Washington (d) Stock home

(39) International who's who has been publishing since

(a) 1947 (b) 1935

(c) 1928 (d) 1937

(40) A compendium of knowledge is known as

(a) Year Book (b) Encyclopaedia

(c) Almanac (d) Directory

(41) Knowledge of recent development is known as

(a) Present knowledge (b) Future knowledge

(c) Current Knowledge (d) Auxiliary knowledge

(42) Who's who of Indian Writers (1961) was published by

(a) Sahitya Academy (b) National Book Trust

(c) Asia publication (d) Oxford Press India

(43) Bibliography is a

(a) List of document (b) List of books

(c) List of serials (d) Trade list

(44) Annals of library science and documentation is a

(a) Book (b) Periodical

(c) Directory (d) Dictionary

(45) Patent Information system of India is established in India in the year of

(a) 1980 (b) 1982

(c) 1985 (d) 1975

(46) Indiana by Sen Gupta is a tool for

(a) Information Technology

(b) Selecting reference sources

(c) Selecting books on India

(d) Selecting periodical publishing in India

(47) Joseph Whitaker name is associated to the field of

(a) Bibliography (b) Almanac

(c) Gazetteer (d) Encyclopaedia

(48) Name the publisher of "Directory of Research Institution in India

(a) DESIDOC (b) SENDOC

(c) NISCAIR (d) NISSAT

(49) Identify from the following which are purely geographical sources

(i) Maps (ii) Atlases

(iii) Encyclopedias (iv) Year books

(a) I, II (b) II IV

(c) I, IV (d) II, III

(50) Information about scale and projection con be found in

(a) Encyclopaedia (b) Hand Book & manuals

(c) Directories (d) Geographical sources

(51) Identify from the following which is an on line reference service

(a) SLIM (b) Ask a Librarian

(c) E-Prints (d) Fax

(52) Who is the publisher of Library Literature & Information Science

(a) H.W. Wilson (b) R.R. Bowker

(c) Vikas Publication (d) Crolior

(53) Identify which are not secondary sources of Information

(i) Bibliography (ii) Dissertation

(iii) Theses (iv) Patents

(a) only I (b) II and III

(c) I II III (d) II III IV

(54) Citation Indexing was first developed in the field of

(a) Mathematics

(b) Library and Information science

(c) Library sciences

(d) Law

(55) Who is the publisher of Indian Library and Information science abstract.

(a) ILA (b) IATLIS

(c) IASLIC (d) LISA

(56) Biological Abstracting periodical has been publishing since

(a) 1907 (b) 1926

(c) 1872 (d) 1976

(57) Information on people, places, capital is to be found in

(a) Encyclopaedia (b) Gazetteer

(c) Digest (d) Quotations

(58) Index Medicus has been publishing since

(a) 1964 (b) 1963

(c) 1967 (d) 1961

(59) Who is the publisher of Guide to Indian periodical literature.

(a) Vikas Publication, New Delhi

(b) NISCAIR, New Delhi

(c) Indian documentation service Gurgoan

(d) H.W Wilson New York

(60) Rajsthan University Library is responsible for the publication

(a) Index India (b) Indian science Index

(c) Subject Index (d) Index of periodical

(61) The producer of Atom Index is

(a) INIS (b) AGRIS

(c) BIOSIS (d) DIALOG

(62) Patent Information system of India is established in the year

(a) 1980 (b) 1982

(c) 1985 (d) 1975

(63) Which of the following are exclusive geographical sources

(i) Maps (ii) Atlases

(iii) Encyclopaedia (iv) Year Books

(a) I & III are correct (b) I & IV are correct

(c) II & III are correct (d) I & II are correct

(64) Herald of Library science publication place is

(a) New Delhi (b) Chennai

(c) Lucknow (d) Kolkata

(65) Who are known as editors of encyclopedia of library and information science

(a) E Richardson

(b) Eugene Garfield

(c) Allen kent and Harrod Lancour

(d) Michel Albert

(66) The systematic list of documents relating to a specific field of knowledge

(a) Author Bibliography

(b) Subject bibliography

(c) National Bibliography

(d) Retrospective conversion

(67) New Encyclopedia Britannica which edition would be last print edition

(a) 13 (b) 14

(c) 15 (d) 16

(68) Trends in Information Management is a biannual journal published by

(a) University of Kashmir

(b) University of Hyderabad

(c) Aligarh Muslim University

(d) Usmania University

(69) The first edition of encyclopaedia Britannica published from

(a) New York (b) London

(c) Chicago (d) Edinburg

(70) Imperial Gazetteer of India, First edition published in

(a) 1881 (b) 1981

(c) 1909 (d) 2005

ANSWERS

(1) b	(2) a	(3) b	(4) c
(5) c	(6) a	(7) b	(8) a
(9) a	(10) a	(11) c	(12) a
(13) b	(14) b	(15) b	(16) a
(17) b	(18) a	(19) d	(20) c
(21) b	(22) a	(23) c	(24) d
(25) a	(26) c	(27) a	(28) d
(29) b	(30) a	(31) b	(32) c
(33) a	(34) b	(35) c	(36) a
(37) c	(38) b	(39) a	(40) b
(41) c	(42) a	(43) b	(44) b
(45) a	(46) b	(47) b	(48) c
(49) d	(50) d	(51) b	(52) a
(53) d	(54) d	(55) c	(56) b
(57) b	(58) a	(59) c	(60) a
(61) a	(62) a	(63) d	(64) c
(65) c	(66) b	(67) c	(68) a
(69) d	(70) a		

4
Information System & Services

(1) A service provided to research scholar in his field and its related field with current information is called

(a) Reference service (b) CAS

(c) Special service (d) Referral service

(2) User profile, is prepared in this service

(a) Current awareness

(b) Selective dissemination of information

(c) Documents delivery of information

(d) Direct service

(3) In a library a service called routing of current periodical to research scholars, comes under

(a) CAS (b) SDI service

(c) Translation service (d) Referral service

(4) Which institute is related to the publication of Mahatma Gandhi bibliography?

(a) SENDOC (b) NASSDOC

(c) NISSAT (d) NISCAIR

(5) Recognize the institute which is merged with INSDOC to form NISCAIR

(a) NICLI (b) NICFOS

(c) NISCOM (d) NICMAP

(6) Association for information management is located at

(a) Rome (b) Tokyo

(c) London (d) New York

(7) Indexing method In which coordination of search term is done at the time of searching, is called

(a) Pre coordinate indexing

(b) Post coordinate indexing

(c) Citation indexing

(d) Indexing by titles

(8) The method of indexing represent full title with entry point is

(a) KWIC (b) KWOC

(c) KWWC (d) WADEX

(9) WADEX refers to

(a) Wide and double index

(b) Wide and described index

(c) Word and author index

(d) With author index

(10) Uniterm index developed by

(a) Derek Austin (b) G Bhattacharya

(c) Mortimer Taube (d) HP Luhn

(11) Role operator are used in the indexing system

(a) POPSI (b) KEY TERM ALFA

(c) Uniterm indexing (d) PRECIS

(12) POPSI application require a no. of steps to perform, these are

(a) 0-8 (b) 1-8

(c) 1-7 (d) 0-7

(13) POSPI is designed by

(a) SR Ranganathan (b) WJ Wilson

(c) Derek Albert (d) None of the above

(14) Match the following

(A) Chain procedure (i) Derek Austin

(B) PRECIS (ii) S.R. Ranganathan

(C) Citation Indexing (iii) Shepard

(D) Keyword Indexing (iv) H.P. Luhn

	A	**B**	**C**	**D**
(a)	I	II	III	IV
(b)	II	III	IV	I
(c)	II	I	III	IV
(d)	II	III	I	IV

(15) In this indexing mechanism card consists holes

(a) Zeta coding (b) KWIC

(c) Batten system (d) Uniterm system

(16) Identify from the following which is not a controlled vocabulary tool

(a) Thesauri (b) Subject heading list

(c) Research tools (d) Classification

(17) BT, NT, RT, term are related to

(a) Catalogue (b) Thesaurus

(c) Reference service (d) Searching terms

(18) Recognize the country which is not a co –operative unit of DEVINSA

(a) Bangladesh (b) Maldives

(c) Japan (d) India

(19) Zatacoding optical coincidence is the example of

(a) Pre-coordinate indexing system

(b) Citation indexing
(c) Permutation indexing
(d) Post coordinate indexing

(20) Calvin moorse introduced
(a) Peek-a-boo
(b) Uniterm indexing system
(c) Science citation indexing system
(d) Zatacoding indexing system

(21) Citation Indexing was first developed in the field of
(a) Mathematics
(b) Library & information system
(c) Library science
(d) Law

(22) In thesaurus BT refers to
(a) Better terms (b) Bit terms
(c) Broader terms (d) Big terms

(23) UGC-infonet was launched in India when ____was/ is the Prime Minister of India
(a) Sri Man Mohan Singh
(b) Dr. V P Singh
(c) Sri Atal Bihari Vajpayee
(d) Sri PV Narsimharav

(24) ALSIB now known (as Association for Information Management) changed its name in the year
(a) 1976 (b) 1927
(c) 1978 (d) 1983

(25) Library association of UK was founded in
(a) 1876 (b) 1977
(c) 1938 (d) 1877

(26) National botanical research institute is situated in
(a) Bangalore (b) Lucknow

(c) Kolkata (d) New Delhi

(27) In which year ENVIS was setup in India

(a) 1992 (b) 1972

(c) 2000 (d) 1982

(28) Identify the full name of the NOPR, a service rendered by NASCAIR

(a) National open process and retrieval

(b) National open periodical research

(c) NISCAIR online periodical repository

(d) NISCAIR online publication resources

(29) Which one of the fallowing organization joined the library association to form CILIP in 2012

(a) Institute of librarianship

(b) Institute of de la documentation

(c) Institute of science and technology

(d) Institute of information scientist

(30) In the studies of cranfield I, the indexing system chosen were

(I) Universal decimal classification scheme

(II) KWIC

(III) KWOC

(IV) An alphabetical subject catalog

(a) Only I and IV (b) Only I and II

(c) Only IV (d) Only III

(31) Cranfield test has been done under the guidance of

(a) HP Latin (b) Mortimer

(c) CW Cleverdon (d) DS Blair

(32) Crainfield studies is done in the field of

(a) Classification

(b) Evolution of manual I R system

(c) Cataloguing of non-Book material

(d) Information storage

(33) To check the efficiency of an indexing system as good what will be the position of Recall and precision

(a) When recall is high, precision will de also high

(b) When recall is low precision will be low

(c) When precision will be high the recall will low

(d) When recall is high precision will be zero

(34) Data centers fulfill the need of

(a) Bibliographic information needs

(b) Numerical data on a subject

(c) Consolidated, evaluated information need

(d) Summary of information

(35) IFLA launched its institutional repository containing papers of world library and information congress, it was launched in the year of

(a) 2013 (b) 2012

(c) 2011 (d) 2010

(36) Institutional repository is the digitized format of

(a) Al academic information of member of institution

(b) All student' information of university

(c) All institution of a subject

(d) Content created by member of an institution

(37) Who has established Indian railway library

(a) F A wheelers (b) A O wheelers

(c) A H wheelers (d) H A wheelers

(38) WIPO is an organisation relate to

(a) Word information protocol organization

(b) World information publication office

(c) World intellectual property organisation

(d) World intellectual priority organisation

(39) PRÉCIS and NESTED phrase indexing system (NEPHIS) are two examples of

(a) Keyword indexing (b) Citation indexing
(c) String indexing (d) Alphabetical indexing

(40) It is a searching technique in an IR system, which implies correction of spelling errors
(a) Truncation searching
(b) Fuzzy searching
(c) Field searching
(d) Manual searching

(41) If the terms are selected from the original document for indexing it is called
(a) Derivative indexing
(b) Descriptive indexing
(c) Assignment indexing
(d) Automatic indexing

(42) In a indexing system term are assigned using a controlled vocabulary, these term are called
(a) Keyword (b) Digital document
(c) Descriptors (d) Titles

(43) Descriptive indexing is also called
(a) Uniterm indexing (b) Citation indexing
(c) Keyword indexing (d) Alphabetical indexing

(44) The proximity searching have 2 operators as
(a) Simple critical (b) WITH and NEAR
(c) Not and or (d) Close and far

(45) IFLA Acronym now stands for
(a) International festival of library association
(b) Information federation of library associative and institution
(c) International federation of library Association and institution
(d) Inter-function of library association

(46) Match the following with their year of origin

(A) ALA (i) 1877

(B) SLA (ii) 1876

(C) ASLIB (iii) 1909

(D) LA (iv) 1924

	A	B	C	D
(a)	I	II	III	IV
(b)	III	II	I	IV
(c)	II	III	IV	I
(d)	III	IV	I	II

(47) AGRIS work at

(a) One level (b) Two level

(c) Three level (d) None of the above

(48) AGRIS works under

(a) IAEA (b) ILO

(c) FAO (d) UNEP

(49) The Head Quarter of AGRIS is at

(a) Vienna (b) USA

(c) Netherlands (d) UK

(50) Relate the following Information centre to their focal point

(A) INIS (i) ENVIS

(B) AGRIS (ii) BARC

(C) INFOTERRA (iii) ARIC

	A	B	C	D
(a)	I	III	II	
(b)	II	I	III	
(c)	II	III	I	

(51) OCLC now known as

(A) Ohio College Library centre

(B) On line computer library centre

(C) On line college library centre

(D) Ohio college language centre

(52) Relate following Indexing method with their originator

(A) Zatacoding	(i) Mortimer Taube
(B) Uniterm Indexing	(ii) Calvin Moorse
(C) Peek-a-boo	(iii) SR Ranganathan
(D) Chain Procedure	(iv) WE Batten

	A	**B**	**C**	**D**
(a)	I	III	II	IV
(b)	II	I	III	IV
(c)	IV	I	II	III
(d)	II	I	IV	III

(53) Indian National scientific documentation centre is now known as

(a) SSDC (b) ASLIB

(c) NCS (d) NISCAIR

(54) Documentation and Research Training centre was established in the year of

(a) 1952 (b) 1962

(c) 1972 (d) 1982

(55) National Information system for science and Technology came into existence in

(a) 1975 (b) 1977

(c) 1972 (d) 1971

(56) CCF II edition is in

(a) 1 volume (b) 4 volume

(c) 3 volume (d) 2 volume

(57) OJAS is a

(a) Gateway of open Journal

(b) Database of Journal

(c) Program of OCLC

(d) A program of INFLIBNET

(58) What is the ISSN for IASLIC Bulletin

(a) 0018-8441 (b) 0018-4881

(c) 0018-1448 (d) 0018-4481

(59) This indexing system is primarily based on the context dependency concept in preparing string of terms

(a) POPSI (b) Citation Indexing

(c) PRECIS (d) Classified Indexing

(60) SENDOC is located

(a) Ahmadabad (b) Hyderabad

(c) Aurangabad (d) Bangalore

(61) Local information Unit is a part of

(a) NISSAT (b) DELNET

(c) INSDOC (d) SENDOC

(62) UAP stands for

(a) Universal Association of Publisher

(b) Universal Availability of publication

(c) Universal Academic program

(d) United Association of Public libraries

(63) From the following which is not a national documentation centre

(a) INSDOC (b) SENDOC

(c) DESIDOC (d) FID

(64) SENDOC was established to fulfill the information needs of

(a) Large Industries

(b) Foreign Industries

(c) Small scale Industries

(d) Major Industries

(65) VINITI was the National scientific Technical Information system of
(a) USA (b) UK
(c) Hungary (d) Former USSR

(66) Information and library network is established by
(a) UGC (b) NIC
(c) NISSAT (d) RRRLF

(67) A national centre related of IISC is now closed it is
(a) INSDOC (b) NISSAT
(c) NCSI (d) NIC

(68) Full name of ARIC
(a) Agra Research Information centre
(b) Agriculture research information centre
(c) Agriculture research International centre
(d) Ayurvedic Research Information centre

(69) Sir Dorabji Tata Graduate School of social work is now known as
(a) National Institute of social science
(b) Tata Institute of social science
(c) Indian Institute of Samaj Vigyan
(d) None of the above

(70) Name the organisation that publishes "Annals of Indian Administration"
(a) NISSAT
(b) ICSSR
(c) Ministry of Public Administration
(d) ICSU

(71) The National Input centre for INIS in India is
(a) ICAR
(b) IAEA
(c) BARC
(d) Ministry of Atomic energy

(72) IFLA was founded in the year of

(a) 1924 (b) 1927

(c) 1933 (d) 1934

(73) This association is mainly for teachers of library and information science

(a) ILA (b) IASLIC

(c) IATLIS (d) UPLA

(74) The concept of 'stopword' list is relevant in the context of

(a) Uniterm indexing (b) Keyword indexing

(c) Citation Indexing (d) Chain Indexing

(75) Identify the name of information scientist who recently passed away (25 Aug 2013)

(a) HP Singh (b) FW Lancaster

(c) William Fredrick (d) A Neelmeghan

(76) INFOTERRA Works in the field of

(a) Human right

(b) Environmental Information system

(c) Technology information system

(d) Nuclear information system

(77) Where is the Head Quarter of INFOTERRA

(a) Peris (b) Geneva

(c) Nairobi (d) USA

(78) SciFinder is a service relate to

(a) Science citation index

(b) Chemical abstract

(c) A journal of science

(d) None of the above

(79) Where is the national institute for intellectual property management situated.

(a) Kolhapur (b) Nasik

(c) New Delhi (d) Nagpur

(80) International Federation for information and documentation (FID) is dissolved in the year of

(a) 1998 (b) 2000

(c) 2002 (d) 2012

(81) In which of the following the term "search strategy" is used

(a) Cataloguing (b) Classification

(c) Indexing (d) Literature Search

(82) Which one from the following is a post coordinate indexing system

(a) POPSI (b) Subject Heading

(c) Uniterm Indexing (d) PRECIS

(83) In we want to search "corporate" and we write 'corpo*' it is called

(a) Star Searching

(b) Alphabatical searching

(c) Right Truncation Search

(d) Proximity search

(84) In which of the following the word "Truncation" is used

(a) Cataloguing (b) Budgeting

(c) Search formulation (d) Notation

(85) Which one indexing system used name of author in indexing system

(a) POPSI (b) PRECIS

(c) WADEX (d) KWIC

(86) Thesaurus for indexing is use for

(a) Alphabetization

(b) Controlled vocabulary

(c) Uncontrolled vocabulary

(d) As a Dictionery

(87) In PRECIS role operator are indicated by

(a) Small letters (b) Capital letters

(c) Numbers (d) Special symbols

(88) Who coined the word "information Retrieval"

(a) H.P. Luhn (b) C.M. Marshal

(c) F.W. Lancaster (d) Calvin Moorse

(89) MeSH is an example of

(a) Abstracting (b) Indexing Journal

(c) Thesaurus (d) Referral service

(90) PRECIS stands for

(a) Post context indexing system

(b) Pre context indexing

(c) Preserved context indexing system

(d) Pre classification system

(91) Which one of the following indexing has been used by BNB to derive subject heading

(a) Chain Procedure (b) LISH

(c) POPSI (d) PRECIS

(92) Identify from the following which in not related to evaluation of Information retrieval system

(a) Recall (b) Precision

(c) Relevance (d) Uniformity

(93) The publisher of Sear's List of subject heading is

(a) RR Bowker (b) Academic Press

(c) HW Wilson (d) Cambridge press

(94) In Which indexing system the card for each searchable term is prepared

(a) POPSI (b) Boolean operator

(c) Uniterm indexing (d) Chain procedure

(95) What is AGROVOC

(a) Library of Agriculture

(b) Database of Agriculture
(c) Agriculture thesaurus
(d) Index of AGRIS

(96) N-LIST is a program of
(a) NISSAT (b) UGC
(c) INFLIBNET (d) DADO

(97) It is Journal of Deptt of Library and Information science-university of Kashmir
(a) ERNET (b) Shodh
(c) TRIM (d) Library Journal

(98) "Towards Paperless Information System" A Book written by
(a) HP Luhn (b) Peter Merhalz
(c) FW Lancaster (d) Tim berner Lee

(99) National centre for science information related to IISC Bangalore
(a) Now opened
(b) Now closed
(c) Now digitized
(d) Now open to student of foreign

(100) Information retrieval word introduced in the year
(a) 1952 (b) 1950
(c) 1951 (d) 1954

(101) Who coined the word Information Literacy
(a) Ranganathan (b) Paul Zurkowaski
(c) D.J. Foskett (d) HP Luhn

(102) What is the right sequence of following according to their association
(a) Information data knowledge
(b) Knowledge data information
(c) Data information knowledge
(d) Data knowledge information

(103) The production of information in large volume is known as

(a) Information growth (b) Information increasing

(c) Well of information (d) Information explosion

(104) N-LIST Refers to

(a) National library and information services infrastructure or scholarly content

(b) National list of science translators

(c) National library information structure

(d) National list of scientist

(105) DA-IICT stands for

(a) Direct admission institute of communication technology

(b) Dhiru Bhai Ambani Institute of Information and communication technology

(c) Diru-Ambani information institute & communication technology

(d) Dual Access institute of Inf. And communication technology

(106) Where is DA-IICT situated

(a) Ghandhi Nagar (b) Bhopal

(c) New Delhi (d) Mumbai

(107) Auto abstracting involves the use of computers

(a) Structure the content of an abstract

(b) Prepare indicative abstract

(c) Pickup significant words

(d) Arrange words in order

(108) All union institute for scientific and technical information (VINITI) was established in

(a) 1952 (b) 1953

(c) 1954 (d) 1956

(109) International information center for crystallography was established of

(a) University of Pune
(b) University of Madras
(c) University of Hyderabad
(d) University of Jammu & Kashmir

(110) What is NICDROM

(a) National centre of Drug
(b) National Information centre on CD-ROM
(c) National Centre for dissertation
(d) National centre for Environment

(111) National Centre on Bibliometrics was established in 1988 at

(a) DRTC (b) NISCAIR
(c) INFLIBNET (d) National Library

(112) National Knowledge Resource consortium is relate to

(a) NISCAIR
(b) University of Delhi
(c) Ministry of Information & Broadcasting
(d) OCLC

ANSWERS

(1) b	(2) b	(3) a	(4) b
(5) c	(6) c	(7) b	(8) b
(9) c	(10) c	(11) d	(12) b
(13) d	(14) c	(15) c	(16) c
(17) b	(18) c	(19) d	(20) d
(21) d	(22) c	(23) c	(24) d
(25) d	(26) b	(27) d	(28) c
(29) d	(30) a	(31) c	(32) b
(33) c	(34) b	(35) a	(36) d
(37) c	(38) c	(39) c	(40) b
(41) a	(42) c	(43) c	(44) b

(45) c	(46) c	(47) b	(48) a
(49) a	(50) c	(51) b	(52) d
(53) d	(54) b	(55) b	(56) d
(57) a	(58) a	(59) c	(60) b
(61) a	(62) b	(63) d	(64) c
(65) d	(66) a	(67) c	(68) b
(69) b	(70) b	(71) c	(72) b
(73) c	(74) b	(75) b	(76) b
(77) c	(78) b	(79) b	(80) c
(81) c	(82) c	(83) c	(84) c
(85) c	(86) b	(87) a	(88) b
(89) c	(90) c	(91) d	(92) d
(93) c	(94) c	(95) c	(96) c
(97) c	(98) c	(99) b	(100) b
(101) b	(102) c	(103) d	(104) a
(105) b	(106) a	(107) c	(108) a
(109) b	(110) b	(111) b	(112) a

5

Management of Libraries and Information Centres

(1) Who is the author of the book entitled "The principles of scientific management"

(a) McGregor (b) Henry Fayol

(c) F.W. Taylor (d) Henry L Gantt

(2) X Theory of Management suggest

(a) Employees need strict control

(b) Employees work willingly

(c) They need motivation

(d) None of the above

(3) Who has developed X and Y theory of management

(a) Abraham Maslow (b) Henry L Gantt

(c) Eton Mayo (d) Douglas McGregor

(4) Span of control refers

(a) Employees control by themselves

(b) Control by manager to subordinate employee

(c) Control by Association of employee

(d) Control by owner

(5) Line organization is also known as

(a) Military type organization
(b) Functional organization
(c) Line and staff organization
(d) None of the above

(6) Line and staff type organization is the combination of
(a) Line and functional type organization
(b) Span of control and delegation of authority
(c) Management by objective
(d) Manager by organization

(7) MBO refers to
(a) Management by opinion
(b) Management by objection
(c) Management by objective
(d) Manager by organization

(8) Who has developed theory of MBO
(a) Monte Carle
(c) Henry A sharp
(b) Peter Drucker
(d) Maslow

(9) DSS helps its managers
(a) To help employee of library
(c) To visit a distance library
(b) For planning and decision making
(d) Improve library services.

(10) Gnatt Chart is used in
(a) Work Analysis
(c) Job opportunity
(b) Relate to salary
(d) As library equipment for reading E book

(11) Critical path method is developed by
(a) Henry L Gantt and Rezer Bishop
(b) William L Wiz and Mathews

(c) Margon R Walker and James E Kelley

(d) US Military Force

(12) PERT is enunciated by

(a) A Razer

(b) Henry Fayol

(c) Library of congress

(d) UN Navy special project officer

(13) 'Seven Lamps of Conduct' refers to

(a) Seven biggest libraries of the world

(b) Ethics of librarianship

(c) Function of special library

(d) Seven authors of library science.

(14) What is the relation between administration & management

(a) Management is greater than administration

(b) Both are equal

(c) Both made policies

(d) Management carries out the policies in action laid down by administration

(15) A shelf list card is the duplication of

(a) Book Index entry (b) Main entry

(c) Added entry (d) See reference entry

(16) Organizing and Direction

(a) Are functions of administration

(c) Are qualities of libraries

(b) Are functions of cataloguing

(d) Are scientific principles of management

(17) In catalogue card no. of pages, size etc are given in this section, known as

(a) Description section (b) Detail section

(c) Imprint Section (d) Collation section

(18) Imprint section of a catalogue card have

(a) Name of author title and edition

(b) ISBN No.

(c) GMD

(d) Name of publisher, publishing place and year of publication

(19) ISBD (S) relates to cataloguing of

(a) Book of sociology (b) Non book material

(c) Monographs (d) Journal & periodicals

(20) Book card is not inserted in book pocket of a book in case of

(a) Printed book

(b) Reference and other non-issue books

(c) Books of current year

(d) old books have an issue pattern

(21) Shelf rectification implies

(a) Reservation of the books

(b) Stock verification

(c) Replace books at their proper place

(d) Shelving of books after processing

(22) Shelf rectification is needed in

(a) Close access library

(b) Open access library

(c) In both close & open access library

(d) None of the above

(23) Pick out the enemy of library books

(a) Silver fish (b) Rehu fish

(c) Tangen fish (d) Golden fish

(24) Which charging system is developed by Nine E Browne.

(a) Newark charging system

(b) Reader's ticked book ticked
(c) Ledger system
(d) None of the above

(25) What is Kardex system
(a) Keeping records of periodicals
(b) Issue and return method
(c) A procedure of stock verification
(d) None of the above

(26) If you want to know the record of lost books which method would you apply yearly
(a) Shelf rectification
(b) Stock verification
(c) Counting current year books
(d) Kardex system

(27) Who has developed the theory of motivation to the employee
(a) Lupans J (b) Peter Cook
(c) Abraham Maslow (d) Peter Druke

(28) What is the sequence of level of management
(a) Middle, Top, Supervisory
(b) Supervisory, Middle, Top
(c) Top, Middle, Supervisory
(d) None of the above

(29) Peter Phyor devised
(a) Zero based budgeting
(b) PPBS
(c) Formula budgeting
(d) Program budgeting

(30) Which card from the following is not included in Ranganathan's Three card system
(a) Check card

(b) Catalogue card

(c) Register card

(d) Classification Index card

(31) ISBD is a program of

(a) UNESCO (c) IFLA

(b) FID (d) ISO

(32) Who has enunciated "British Library Music catalog"

(a) EJ Coats (b) DJ Forkett

(c) BC Victory (d) J Mills

(33) For book selection theory who said "best reading for the largest no at the least cost"

(a) Dr. S.R. Ranganathan

(b) Drury

(c) McColvin

(d) Melvil Deway

(34) The number of principles are of management identified by Henry Fayol was

(a) Eight (b) Fourteen

(c) Sixteen (d) Seventeen

(35) Cost benefit analysis means

(a) Performance evaluation based on cost

(b) Performance evaluation based on opening cost

(c) Performance evaluation based on closing cost

(d) Performance evaluation based on benefit

(36) Prepration of budget for the library that recently open comes under

(a) Performance budgeting

(c) PPBS

(b) Zero based budgeting

(d) Line item budget

(37) 'Unity is strength' is one of the principles laid down by

(a) Bernard (b) Taylor
(c) Fayol (d) S.R. Ranganathan

(38) Every Library selects a page in each book for writing accession no. with library seal is known as
(a) Recto page (b) Verso page
(c) Secret page (d) None of the above

(39) Who is called the father of scientific management
(a) Henry Fayol (b) FW Taylor
(c) McColvin (d) J.S. Mill

(40) PPBS is the combination of
(a) Formula Budgeting and line item
(b) Zero based budgeting & line item
(c) Program budgeting and performance budgeting
(d) Program budgeting and zero based

(41) Kaoru Ishikaba is known for its contribution in
(a) TQM (b) PPBS
(c) Formula budgeting (d) Program budgeting

(42) Esprit de corps is one of the principle of scientific management emphasis on
(a) Division of labour (b) Scalar chain
(c) Inspiration (d) Team sprit

(43) Book review is a good source for
(a) Classification of books
(b) Book selection
(c) Digitization
(d) Reference of Article

(44) One of the methods of financial estimation is
(a) Programme method (b) Regular method
(c) Zero based method (d) Per capita method

(45) In India two charging system are very popular, one is Browne charging system other is

(a) Ranganathan charging system
(b) Newark charging system
(c) Modern charging system
(d) Computerized section

(46) Conscience box is related to
(a) Cataloguing section (b) Reference section
(c) Circulation section (d) Librarian desk

(47) Who coined the word POSPORB
(a) Henry Fayol (b) Max Weber
(c) Gulick and Urwik (d) Wilson and Tauber

(48) While entering the library the personal belongings of a reader is kept in
(a) Clock room (b) Gate counter
(c) Property counter (d) Store room

(49) Out dated and rare used books are withdrawn from the library is known as
(a) Weeding (b) Shelving
(c) Stock rectification (d) Stock verification

(50) Financial requirement of a library can be known by various method. Trace out from the following which is not a method of financial estimation
(a) Per Capita Method
(b) Proportional Method
(c) Method of Expenditure
(d) Method of detail

ANSWERS

(1) c	(2) b	(3) d	(4) d
(5) a	(6) a	(7) c	(8) c
(9) c	(10) a	(11) c	(12) d
(13) b	(14) d	(15) b	(16) a
(17) d	(18) d	(19) d	(20) b
(21) c	(22) b	(23) a	(24) d

(25) a	(26) b	(27) c	(28) c
(29) a	(30) b	(31) b	(32) a
(33) d	(34) b	(35) a	(36) b
(37) c	(38) c	(39) a	(40) c
(41) a	(42) d	(43) b	(44) d
(45) b	(46) c	(47) c	(48) c
(49) a	(50) c		

6
Libraries And Society

(1) 'Information is recorded & communicative knowledge' which of the following is not applicable for information

(a) Gained by experience

(b) Gained through experiment

(c) Gained by processing the data

(d) By only collecting facts

(2) Recognize from the following which is not the era of information development

(a) Discipline oriented era

(b) Problem oriented era

(c) Investigation oriented era

(d) Mission oriented era

(3) Library is a growing organism this law emphasis the development is in

(i) Library collection (ii) Library hours

(iii) Library staff (iv) Library Reader

(a) Only I and II (b) Only I and IV

(c) I, II, III (d) I, III, IV

(4) Which of the following is not a method of library extension service

(a) Story hours for children
(b) Computer game
(c) Cultural program
(d) Mobile library service

(5) Saraswati Mahal Library is situated at
(a) Chennai (b) Koyambatoor
(c) Tanjore (d) Kashmir

(6) Which was the first unofficial public library, open to the public
(a) Saraswati Mahal library
(b) Asiatic society library, Bengal
(c) Fort Williom college library
(d) Royal library of Tipoo Sultan

(7) Asiatic society of Bengal was founded by
(a) Tipoo Sultan (b) Babar
(c) Sir Willian Jones (d) Messrs Cook

(8) Asiatic society of Bengal was Formed in
(a) 1764 (c) 1864
(b) 1784 (d) 1774

(9) Calcutta Public library was set up in
(a) 1784 (c) 1790
(b) 1835 (d) 1836

(10) In 1903 Culcutta Public library merged with
(a) Khudabaksh Library (c) Oriental Library
(b) Imperial Library (d) Connemara Library

(11) Dr. Ranganathan presented a draft model library act in a conference. The name of the conference was
(a) All India Conference
(b) Conference for public libraries
(c) First All Asia Educational Conference
(d) Library of congress Conference

(12) Who appoints the Librarian of library of congress

(a) Library committee

(b) President of USA

(c) By the Public of USA

(d) By education institution

(13) Cataloguing in source is an example of

(a) Inter library loan

(b) Centralized cataloguing

(c) LC card

(d) None of the above

(14) In cataloguing in source full catalogue entry is printed on

(a) Pages of last in a book

(b) Verso of the title page

(c) Blank page

(d) Back of the book

(15) What was the "Farmington Plan" of USA in acquisition policy

(a) Purchase of library furniture

(b) Purchase of foreign publication

(c) Purchase of library cards

(d) Purchase of resources for library

(16) This centre uses converted from regional co-operative network to national network

(a) MEDLARS

(c) OCLC

(b) Cambridge University

(d) NISSAT

(17) Ohio College Library centre founded in

(a) 1924 (b) 1929

(c) 1967 (d) 1977

(18) JANET stands for

(a) Join Army network

(b) Joint Academic Network

(c) Joint Access Network

(d) Journal access network

(19) Open access system is primary requirement for the implementation of

(a) First law (b) Third law

(c) Fifth law (d) Both a and b

(20) Relate the following institution with their place

(A) Nalanda (i) Gujarat

(B) Takshasila (ii) Bhagalpur Bihar

(C) Villabhi (iii) Bihar

(D) Vikramashila (iv) Punjab province in Pakistan

	A	B	C	D
(a)	III	II	I	IV
(b)	II	III	IV	I
(c)	IV	I	III	II
(d)	I	III	II	IV

(21) Ratnasagara is a name associated with

(a) An ocean (b) Library of Nalanda

(c) Library of Egypt (d) Ocean of Jwels

(22) Sam pitroda was the chairman of

(a) Education commission

(b) Information commission

(c) National Knowledge commission

(d) Library commission

(23) IASLIC was formed in

(a) 1950 (b) 1955

(c) 1963 (d) 1933

(24) Indian celebrate library day on

(a) 12 August (b) 10 August
(c) 27 September (d) 14 November

(25) Library Week is celebrated between
(a) 14-20 August (b) 14-20 September
(c) 14-20 October (d) 14-20 November

(26) ASLIB was formed in
(a) 1926 (b) 1924
(c) 1933 (d) 1941

(27) The year in which ILA was set up
(a) 1924 (b) 1928
(c) 1931 (d) 1933

(28) Where is Khudabaksh Oriental Library situated
(a) Calcutta (b) New Delhi
(c) Patna (d) Lucknow

(29) Berne Convection is related to
(a) Copy right act at national level
(b) Copy right Act at International level
(c) Copy right Act for Asian countries
(d) None of the above.

(30) ISKO founded in
(a) 1990 (b) 1999
(c) 2002 (d) 1989

(31) Universal copyright convention is developed by
(a) UNESCO (c) UGC
(b) IFLA (d) Library of congress

(32) Golden Jublee year of UGC celeberated in
(a) 2002 (b) 2000
(c) 2001 (d) 2005

(33) RTI is not applicable in
(a) Goa (b) Maharashtra
(c) Mizoram (d) Jammu & Kashmir

(34) Information Technology Act passed in the year of

(a) 1998 (b) 2000

(c) 2001 (d) 2002

(35) Million Book project is a

(a) Acquisition of one Million book in a library

(b) Catalogue of OCLC

(c) Project of Library of Congress

(d) Book digitization project at Universal level

(36) Which committee has recommended NET eligibility essential for being Lecturer, Assistant Librarian and college librarian

(a) Review committee (c) Lal Committee

(b) Mehrotra Committee (d) None of the above

(37) Madras Library Association was founded

(a) 1929 (b) 1928

(c) 1933 (d) 1951

(38) In UNESCO/PGI, PGI refers to

(a) International granting program

(b) Information of government publication

(c) General Information program

(d) Government Information program

(39) Who was the first librarian of national library of India

(a) Dr. S.R. Ranganathan

(b) B.S. Keshuan

(c) C. Majumdar

(d) G. Bhattacharya

(40) Who is responsible for the publication of Indian library & Information Science Abstract

(a) ILA (b) NISSAT

(c) NISCAIR (d) IASLIC

(41) Expansion service is a special feature of

(a) Academic Library (b) Public Library

(c) Special library (d) Digital library

(42) Provide the sequence to the following act according to the year of their enactment

(I) Manipur public library act

(II) Andhra Pradesh library act

(III) Arunachal Pradesh public library act

(IV) West Bengal public library act

(a) III, I, II, IV (b) I, II, III, IV

(c) II, IV, I, III (d) II, III, IV, I

(43) Imperial library is now known as

(a) Kolkata public library

(b) National library

(c) Academic library

(d) State central library

(44) Who had invited American Librarian Willian Allenson Borden to India

(a) Maharaja Sayaji Rav Goekwad II

(b) Lord Curzon

(c) Maharaja Sayaji Rav Goekwad III

(d) None of the above

(45) Which sequence is correct of following association according to their year of origin in ascending order

(a) SLA, ALA, ILA (b) ILA, ALA, SLA

(c) ALA, SLA, ILA (d) ALA, ILA, SLA

(46) The first right to information (RTI) library in Asia is established at

(a) New Delhi (b) Kranchi

(c) Mumbai (d) Chandigarh

(47) Name the library that is recently inaugurated by Malala Yousafzai, A human right activist

(a) Central library of Japan
(b) School library in new Jersey
(c) Children library in New York
(d) New Birmingham library

(48) Manifesto for public libraries was prepared by
(a) UNFSCO (b) FID
(c) ALA (d) Library of congress

(49) A national body which provide financial support to public libraries in India is
(a) UGC (b) NISSAT
(c) RRRLF (d) INSDOC

(50) Recognize from the following which concept is not a type of the information
(a) Empirical information
(b) Typical information
(c) Procedural Information
(d) Stimulatory information

(51) Shannon and Weaver is associated with
(a) Information International
(b) Communication Model
(c) Distance Learning
(d) Marketing of information

(52) What is EATPUT model
(a) A model for analyzing Information system
(b) A model for information seeking behaviour
(c) A model for book selection
(d) A model for recording of serials

(53) Who has devised EAT PUT model
(a) Anthony William (b) Anthony Debons
(c) Anthony Clark (d) Antony Robert

(54) Recognize from the following which right is not included in Intellectual property rights

(i) Patent right (ii) Fundamental right

(iii) Copy right (iv) Human right

(a) I and II only (b) I and III only

(c) II and IV only (d) I and IV only

(55) RTI came into force on

(a) June 2005 (b) 10 October 2005

(c) 13 October 2005 (d) May 2005

(56) First library school in world is established in

(a) Oxford university (b) Stanford university

(c) Columbia University (d) University of Chicago

(57) Library Legislation helps in

(a) Improving library service

(b) Preparing library software

(c) Inter Library loan

(d) Assistance in book selection

(58) Most of the public library use

(a) Colon classification

(b) Dewey decimal classification

(c) Universal Decimal classification

(d) Library of congress

(59) Who was the first president of Madras Library Association

(a) S.R. Ranganathan

(b) K.V. Krishanaswamy

(c) B.K. Keshvan

(d) Sarvpalli Radhakrishanan

(60) What is the old name of Annamalai University

(a) St. Stephen College (b) Queens Merry College

(c) Meenakshi College (d) Lakshmi College

(61) ILA has developed a database of libraries which is called

(a) Takshshila (b) Soul

(c) OASIS (d) Nalanda

(62) A School library inculcates .... among the school children

(a) Saving habit (b) Competition habit

(c) Reading habit (d) Speaking boldly

(63) Karnataka Public library act was enacted in the year

(a) 1965 (b) 1967

(c) 1979 (d) 1988

(64) It is an oldest form of library cooperation

(a) Library Network (b) Inter Library loan

(c) Resource shairing (d) Consortia

(65) In which university M. Lib & I.S. Course was first started

(a) Aligarh Muslim University

(b) BHU

(c) Delhi University

(d) Madras University

(66) Who was awarded First Ph.D. in Library science

(a) Pandeya S.K. Sharma

(b) P.N. Kaula

(c) J.S. Sharma

(d) D.B. Krishnarao

(67) Which university was first awarded Ph.D. degree in library science

(a) Aligarh University (b) BHU

(c) Madras University (d) Delhi University

(68) RRRLE works under the ministry of

(a) Education

(b) Culture

(c) Information and Broadcasting

(d) Urban affairs

(69) In India ISBN is provided by

(a) National Book Trust (b) National Library

(c) INSDOC (d) RRRLF

(70) In ISBN the No. 81 refers to code for

(a) Japan (b) USA

(c) India (d) London

(71) UGC came in to existence in

(a) December 1951 (b) December 1953

(c) January 1949 (d) January 1950

(72) Who was the chairman of "Committee on National Network System for University/Libraries (1988)"

(a) R.C. Malhotra (b) Dr. Ranganathan

(c) Prof. Yashpal (d) D.S. Kothari

(73) Who was the first chair person of UGC

(a) Dr. Sarvapalli Radhakrishanan

(b) Dr. Rajendra Prasad

(c) C.D. Deshmukh

(d) S. Krishnachari

(74) IGNOU was established in India

(a) 1975 (b) 1985

(c) 1986 (d) 1988

(75) According to new amendments in copy right law in India, copy right is granted for

(a) Fifty years after the book is published

(b) Fifty years after the death of author

(c) Sixty years after the book is published

(d) Sixty years after the death of author

(76) NAAC Stands for

(a) National Accreditation and Authority council

(b) Northern accreditation authority committee

(c) National assessment and accreditation council

(d) Northern Assessment and accreditation council

(77) 'Union list' is a record of

(a) Persons living in Union territory

(b) Periodical available in a group of libraries

(c) Library unions located in a union territory

(d) Union of library members

(78) Which library is authorized to receive books under 'Delivery of Books Act'?

(a) National science library Delhi

(b) National law library

(c) State central library Mumbai

(d) Parliament library, Delhi

(79) What is project Gutenberg

(a) Library consortia (b) Project of Inflibnet

(c) Free e-books (d) Private network

(80) Connemarra Public library was established in

(a) 1976 (b) 1800

(c) 1896 (d) 1850

ANSWERS

(1) d	(2) c	(3) d	(4) b
(5) c	(6) b	(7) c	(8) c
(9) d	(10) c	(11) c	(12) b
(13) b	(14) b	(15) b	(16) b
(17) c	(18) b	(19) d	(20) a
(21) b	(22) c	(23) b	(24) a
(25) d	(26) b	(27) d	(28) c
(29) b	(30) d	(31) a	(32) a
(33) d	(34) b	(35) d	(36) c
(37) b	(38) c	(39) b	(40) d
(41) b	(42) c	(43) b	(44) a
(45) c	(46) d	(47) d	(48) a

(49) c	(50) b	(51) b	(52) a
(53) b	(54) c	(55) c	(56) c
(57) a	(58) b	(59) b	(60) c
(61) d	(62) c	(63) b	(64) b
(65) c	(66) d	(67) d	(68) b
(69) d	(70) c	(71) b	(72) c
(73) c	(74) b	(75) d	(76) c
(77) b	(78) c	(79) c	(80) c

7

Research Methodology & Statistical Analysis

(1) What is research
- (a) A method to obtain solution of the problem
- (b) A descriptive method to obtain solution of the problem
- (c) A systematic method to obtain solution of the problem
- (d) A systematic method to obtain tentative solution of the problem

(2) Historical method of research can be applied
- (a) Only in History
- (b) Only in Arts subject
- (c) In science subject
- (d) In all subject

(3) Scientific method of research can be used
- (a) Only in science
- (b) Only in social sciences
- (c) Only in natural science
- (d) In all subjects

(4) Experimental method of research is same as
- (a) Historical method
- (b) Case study
- (c) Scientific method
- (d) Statistical method

(5) Research is meant for which of the following

(a) Searching facts

(b) Searching data

(c) Searching information

(d) Searching facts and their meaning

(6) "Case study method may be defined as a small inclusive and intensive study of an individual in which the investigation brings to bear all his skill and methods, or as a systematic gathering of enough information about a person to permit one to understand how he or she function as unit of society" Who said this statement in the reference of case study

(a) Good and Halt (b) H.P. Young

(c) D.N. Shrivastava (d) None of the above

(7) A tentative solution of a problem by a researcher is known as

(a) Variable (b) Principle

(c) Result (d) Hypothesis

(8) Which statement is not matched with research

(a) Research gain new knowledge

(b) Research is purposive

(c) Research is personally biased

(d) Research is logical and objective

(9) A plan of study, which an investigator makes and does the work accordingly is known as

(a) Research problem (b) Research Design

(c) Research in hand (d) Solution

(10) Conducting research in a field what will be the first step in research process

(a) Collection of data

(b) Comparison of variable

(c) Selection of research problem
(d) Research description

(11) Which type of process research is
(a) Mechanical (b) Mental
(c) Intellectual (d) Semi mechanical

(12) Pure research is an investigation conducted by
(a) An individual (b) An organisation
(c) A group of teachers (d) Two persons

(13) Inductive research proceeds from
(a) General to particular
(b) Particular to general
(c) Particular to particular
(d) General to general

(14) Deductive research proceeds from
(a) General to particular
(b) Particular to general
(c) General to general
(d) None of the above

(15) Which type of process inductive logic is
(a) Theory is developed by observing many individual example
(b) Theory of formula
(c) Principles of research
(d) Theory is developed by observing all phenomena

(16) Which type of process deductive logic is
(a) Theory is tested
(b) Theory is tested by principles
(c) Theory is tested by known scientific principles
(d) Theory is not tested.

(17) Statistical method in research is applied to obtain
(a) Facts

(b) Interpretation of numerical data
(c) Real observation
(d) Deduced facts

(18) Collection of data is done by — method
(a) One method (b) Two method
(c) Various method (d) Four method

(19) The data is of two kinds, these are
(a) Rural and urban data
(b) Primary and Secondary data
(c) Primary and Testing data
(d) Current and primary data

(20) Identify from the following which is a method of data collection
(a) School (c) Committee
(b) Interview (d) University

(21) The procedure of interview in which a frame work of questions are prepared in written form is known as
(a) Structure interview (b) Focussed Interview
(c) Specific Interview (d) Central interview

(22) In this type of interview method certain sets of data are collected about a large no. of persons, known as
(a) Qualitative interview
(b) Quantitative interview
(c) Observation of interviewer
(d) Data interpretation

(23) "Law of Scattering" was propounded by
(a) B.C. Vickery (b) Stevens
(c) P.V. Young (d) Bradford

(24) An approach to social investigation with full and active participation of the community in the research

process is known as

(a) Statistical study (b) Sociometric research

(c) Projective technique (d) Participatory research

(25) Who are both consumers and producers of information

(a) Teachers (b) Courts

(c) Researchers (d) Journals.

(26) What will be the mean of the series of following number 2, 4, 6, 8, 7, 9

(a) 6 (b) 8

(c) 7 (d) 36

(27) What will be the median of following series of number 4, 8, 12, 9, 8, 7

(a) 48 (b) 29

(c) 29.5 (d) 30

(28) What will be the mode of following no series 8, 7, 8, 6, 8, 6, 8, 6

(a) 8 (b) 6

(c) 7 (d) 0

(29) When hypothesis is stated negatively it is called

(a) Positive hypothesis (b) Conceptual hypothesis

(c) Null Hypothesis (d) Universal Hypothesis

(30) An Entity in scientific investigation may change its quantity or quality is known as

(a) Hypotheses (c) Variable

(b) Clause (d) Observation

(31) Identify from the following which method is not a method of research

(a) Historical method (b) Classification method

(c) Descriptive method (d) Field study method

(32) Action Research is

(a) Defendant on policy

(b) Immediate solution of a problem
(c) Quasi Research
(d) None of the above

(33) If a psychologist, studies the behaviour of a mentally retried child, this type of research is known as

(a) Analytical method (b) Case study
(c) Field study (d) Variable study

(34) "Scientific method refers to techniques employed by scientists in pursuit of knowledge" who said

(a) Chaplin (b) W.C.B Sayers
(c) Ranganathan (d) Margrett mann

(35) Which is not a characteristic of scientific method

(a) Verifiability (b) Systematic study
(c) Random decision (d) Generalization

(36) Systematically arrange the following steps of scientific method of research

(i) Hypothesis
(ii) Generalization
(iii) Collection of data
(iv) Selection of the problem

(a)	I	II	III	IV
(b)	II	III	IV	I
(c)	IV	I	III	II
(d)	IV	I	II	III

(37) From the following which is not a tool of data collection

(a) Questionnaire (b) Legislation
(c) Interview (d) Observation

(38) Ex-post facto design is a

(a) Selection of problem of research
(b) Formation of Hypotheses

(c) A form of experimental design
(d) None of the above

(39) It is a technique of research
(a) Referral (b) Content Analysis
(c) Analytic-synthetic (d) Observation

(40) It is a research design, analysis event from present to past
(a) Diagnostic design
(b) Exploratory design
(c) Ex-post- facto design
(d) Content analysis

(41) Lotka law was propounded in
(a) 1924 (b) 1926
(c) 1930 (d) 1938

(42) Bradford law came into existence in
(a) 1934 (b) 1924
(c) 1926 (d) 1948

(43) Zipf's low is enunciated in
(a) 1949 (b) 1939
(c) 1950 (d) 1967

(44) Hulme coined the word
(a) Bibliometrics
(b) Statistical Bibliography
(c) Script
(d) Social Bibliography

(45) Bibliometric word was coined in 1969, by
(a) FW Lancaster (b) S.C. Bradford
(c) A Prichard (d) Peter William

(46) In research process any entity that can change its quantity and quality is known as
(a) Research problem (b) Hypothesis

(c) Variable (d) Researchers

(47) In research process the variable controlled by researcher is called

(a) Independent variable

(b) Dependent variable

(c) Intervenity variable

(d) Organismic variable

(48) The research conducted is keeping in view knowledge for the sake of knowledge in called

(a) Behavioural Research

(b) Fundamental Research

(c) Applied Research

(d) Action Research

(49) To know the TRP (Television Rating Point) of a channel the research is conduced, based on

(a) User's Interaction (b) Sample survey

(c) By a test (d) Interview

(50) The best method of testing hypothesis is

(a) Survey method

(b) Historical method

(c) Laboratory experiment

(d) Field study

(51) Two method of generalization are

(i) Logical method (ii) Priority method

(iii) Secondary method (iv) Statistical method

(a) Only I, II (b) II, III

(c) I, IV (d) III, IV

(52) Pick out the method that relates to the methods of sampling

(i) Judgement or purposive sampling

(ii) Quato sampling

(iii) Universal sampling

(iv) Cluster Sampling

(a) I, II, III (b) I, IV

(c) I, II, III (d) I, II, IV

(53) Observation depends on three elements

(a) Seeing, noticing, speaking

(b) Watching noticing perception

(c) Sensation, attention perception

(d) Sensation, reading perception

(54) When a researcher mix-ups with a group of people he wants to observe for their activities is called

(a) Subjective observation

(b) Participant observation

(c) Cultural observation

(d) Simple observation

(55) Research is done by

(i) Acquiring fact

(ii) Re-interpreat old theories

(iii) Rewrite old theories

(iv) Computerize theories

(a) Only IV (b) Only I

(c) I and II (d) I and IV

(56) Σx^2—— is the formula of counting N

(a) Mean (b) Mode

(c) SD (d) Scaling

(57) Spiral of scientific method has four cardinal point, there are

(a) Correlation, concept, Nadir, ascendant

(b) Concreteness, conceptualization, ascendant, regression

(c) Nadir, Ascendant, Zenith, Descendent

(d) Nadir, Zenith, Bibliography, hypothesis

(58) On spiral of scientific method, the cardinal point Nadir to Ascendant contains

(a) Fundamental Laws (b) Deduced laws

(c) Basic Laws (d) Empirical laws

(59) On spiral of scientific method fundamental laws are found

(a) Zenith to descendant

(b) Descendant to Nadir

(c) Nadir to ascendant

(d) Ascendant to Zenith

(60) Lotka law is based on

(a) Frequency of publication of authors

(b) Frequency of words

(c) Counting of cited journals by other

(d) None of the above

(61) Barchart, Pie chart and Histogram are examples of

(a) Textual Representation

(b) Resonses

(c) Verbal representation

(d) Graphic picture

(62) In Research methodology schedules are used for

(a) Presenting hypothesis

(b) Data collection

(c) Research design

(d) Define the problem

(63) The form of data collection containing question or tables filled by researcher after getting information from the informants is called

(a) Questionnaire (b) Schedules

(c) Review (d) Sociometry

(64) In this form of data collection researcher do not have direct contact to respondent

(a) Questionnaire (b) Schedules

(c) Observation (d) None of the above

(65) Pauline V young is related to the field of

(a) Classification

(b) Reference service

(c) Research Methodology

(d) Mathematics

(66) The person who is taking interview is called

(a) Spoke person (b) Interviewer

(c) Interviewee (d) Orator

(67) A person who is facing interview is called

(a) Interrogator (b) Interviewer

(c) Interviewee (d) Informer

(68) Action Research is also known as

(a) Active research (b) Applied research

(c) Processed research (d) Documentary research

(69) The difference between the sample estimates and the true population estimate is known as

(a) Good sampling (b) Samplc error

(c) Systematic sampling(d) None of the above

(70) Which quality research worker should not have?

(a) Knowledge of the subject

(b) Biased attitude

(c) Knowledge of technique of reserve

(d) Imagination.

(71) The sampling frame are

(a) Structure of received information

(b) List, Index containing population records

(c) List of some principles to be followed

(d) Advance stage of sampling

(72) Identify which is not a sampling technique

(a) Random sampling (b) Marginal sampling

(c) Multi stage sampling(d) Quota sampling

(73) Quota sampling is mainly used in

(a) Student's behaviour in large

(b) Marketing research and election polls

(c) Production of crop

(d) None of the above

(74) Identify from the following which is not a research design

(a) Descriptive design (b) Exploratory design

(c) Complex Design (d) Experimental Design

(75) What is content Analysis research

(a) Analysis problem of social life

(b) Explain social contact

(c) Related to content

(d) None of the Above

ANSWERS

(1) d	(2) d	(3) a	(4) c
(5) d	(6) b	(7) d	(8) c
(9) b	(10) c	(11) c	(12) a
(13) b	(14) a	(15) a	(16) c
(17) b	(18) c	(19) b	(20) c
(21) a	(22) b	(23) d	(24) d
(25) c	(26) a	(27) c	(28) a
(29) c	(30) b	(31) b	(32) b
(33) b	(34) a	(35) c	(36) c
(37) b	(38) b	(39) b	(40) c
(41) b	(42) a	(43) a	(44) b
(45) c	(46) c	(47) a	(48) b
(49) b	(50) c	(51) c	(52) d
(53) c	(54) b	(55) c	(56) c

(57) c	(58) d	(59) d	(60) a
(61) d	(62) b	(63) b	(64) b
(65) b	(66) b	(67) c	(68) b
(69) b	(70) b	(71) b	(72) b
(73) c	(74) c	(75) a	

8
Library Acts in India

1	Madras Public Library Act Called Tamil Nadu Act	1948
2	Andhra Pradesh Public Library Act	1960
3	Karnataka Public Library Act	1965
4	Maharashtra Public Library Act	1967
5	West Bengal Public Library Act	1979
6	Manipur Public library Act	1988
7	Kerala Public Library Act	1989
8	Haryana Public Library Act	1989
9	Mizoram Public Library Act	1993
10	Goa Public Library Act	1993
11	Gujarat Public Library Act	2001
12	Orissa Public Library Act	2001
13	Uttaranchal Public Library Act	2005
14	Uttar Pradesh Public Library Act	2005
15	Rajasthan Public Library Act	2006
16	Bihar Public Library Act	2007
17	Pondicherry Public Library Act	2007/2008
18	Chhattisgarh Public Library Act	2008
19	Arunachal Pradesh Public Library Act	2009

9
Abbreviations and Acronyms

ADINE	Ahmadabad Library Network
APINESS	Asia Pacific Information Network in social sciences
ASTINFO	Regional Network of the exchange of information and experience in Asia and the pacific
ASTM	American Society for Testing of Material
BIOSIS	Bioscience Information Service
BLAISE	British Library Automated Information service
BTIS	Biotechnology Information system
CASSI	Chemical Abstract Service Source Index
CERN	The European centre for nuclear research
CORD	Centre for occupational research and development
CSNET	Computer science network
DEVSIS	Development science information system
DMCA	Digital Millennium copyright Act
ERIC	Education resources information centre
ERNET	Education Research Network

FRAD	Functional Requirement for Authority Data
FRBR	Functional Requirement for Bibliographic Records
FRSAD	Functional Requirement for subject Authority data
IAEA	International Atomic Energy Agency
IMCE	International Meeting of Cataloguing Experts
INDEST	Indian National Digital Library in Engineering, Science and Technology
INFOTERRA	International Referral system for sources of environmental information
INIS	International Nuclear Information system
ISDN	Integrated Service digital Network
JANET	Joint Academy Network
MARBI	Machine Readable Bibliographic Information
NCSI	National centre for science information
NDLTD	The Networked Digital Library of Thesis and Dissertation
OAI-PMH	Open Archive Initiative- Protocol for Metadata harvesting
OECD	Operation for economic cooperation and development
RFID	Radio frequency Identification
RINSA	Regional Information Network for south and central Asia
SIS	Society for Information science
SMEER	Society for Applied Microwave electronic engineering and research

TECHNONET ASIA	An Asian Network for Industrial Technology and extension
VPN	Virtual Private Network

10
New Concepts and Emerging Trends

(I) META DATA

Metadata can be defined in two different ways-

1. Description provided for networked information and digital resources by following a standard or framework (eg. Dublin core) that is specifically created for this purpose
2. It includes cataloguing and indexing data created for any kind of documents by using traditional methods for describing and organising information. So cataloguing data produce by using AACR2 and DDC is also regarded as metadata.

HTML tags or hyperlinks can also be metadata for digital environment.

Metadata standard

Dublin core and RDF (Resource description Framework) are example of metadata standard.

(II) DUBLIN CORE (DC)

Dublin core is a simple content description model for electronic resources. In Dublin core workshop by various expert from the library world, the networking and digital library research communities and a variety of content specialists were gathered and created jointly Dublin core metadata. Dublin core consists 15 elements.

1. Title
2. Creator
3. Subject
4. Description
5. Publisher
6. Contributor
7. Date
8. Type
9. Format
10. Identifier
11. Source
12. Language
13. Relation
14. Coverage
15. Right

In practice, Dublin core is mainly used to provide simple descriptions for networked resources like websites.

(III) RESOURCE DESCRIPTION FRAMEWORK (RDF)

RDF is based upon the idea making statement about the resources (Particularly web resources) in the form of subject, predicate and object expression.

For e.g. the library have books on Biochemistry

Subject	-	Library
Predicate	-	Books
Object	-	Biochemistry

This expression is known as triples in RDF terminology. RDF relate to W3C (World Wide Web consortia) specification originally designed as metadata

data model.

Web 2.0 : It allows its user not only to read the web pages but also to contribute your efforts in providing reliable content to everyone in a user friendly way. In other words it allows contribution of user for updating information & service that may be useful to new user.

Library 2.0 : The term "library 2.0" was coined by Michael Casey on his Blog Library Crunch Casey suggested that libraries at a crossword where many of the elements of Web2.0 have applicable value within library community both in technology based services and in non technology based services .In other words library 2.0 allows its user creat content and change content with reliable environment . According To Wikipedia " Library 2.0 is a loosly defined model for a modernized form of library services that reflecta transition within the library world in the way that services are delivered to users. The focus is on the user centered change and participation in the creation of content and community .This include on line services like the use of OPAC system and an increased flow of information from the user back to the library."

Dataware House : Dataware house is a place where data is stored for archival, analysis and security purposes. A dataware house is central repository of an organisation or business,

The term data ware house was coined by W.H. Inmon. IBM uses the term information ware house. Usually a data ware house is either a single computer or many computers (servers) tied together to create one giant. Computer system.

Data Mart : Data mart are similar or less integrated data housing. They are the database of just one division of business eg. Record of sales data.

Index Translationum : World Bibliography of translation. It is a list of books translated in the world. The index translationum was created in 1932. The database contains cumulative bibliographic information on books, translated & published in about 100 of UNESCO member states since 1929.

Descipline included are literature social and human science, Natural & exact science, Art, History and so on. The database is updated regularly.

SCONUL : (Society college, Nation and University Libraries) It include libraries of UK and Ireland SCONUL promots awareness of the role of academic libraries in supporting research excellence and student achievement and employlibility.

ACRL : (Association of college and Research Libraries) ACRL is a division of American library association. It is a professional association of academic librarians and other interested individuals. It is dedicated to enhancing the ability of Academic Libraries and information professionals to serve the information needs of higher education community and to improve learning teaching and research.

On Line IR System : On line system also known as online database the word database is used for the system. DIALOG and MEDLINE are two example of online IR system.

Online system allows the user to search databases located remotely with the help of computer and telecommunication technology. Initially the system supported only batch mode (i.e. an individual search request is not processed immediately after its submission but until a certain number of request have been assembled) and later introduced real time interaction between user and system.

Now full text information included in only system is selected and represented by professionals. The information professional work as an intermediaries between the system and the user with information needs as system cannot be used by trial and error method it needs training before using it.

Wall Picture Principle : "If two facts A and B of a subject are such that the concept behind B will not be operative unless the concept behind A is conceded, same as without wall we can not draw picture ex. In "cure' is not operative unless the concept behind the term disease is conceded" (Prolegomena).

In this case wall picture principle has determining that the round to which the concept 'Disease' should be assigned as the one preceding the emerging facet 'cure'.

Whole Organ Principle : If in a subject facet "B" is an organ of facet "A" then A should precede B. (Prolegomena P. 427) simply it state if there are two entity, one is the organ of whole. The whole entity come first in facet sequence. Ex. Indian parliament.

The sequence will be India – parliament as parliament is an organ of India.

Cow – Calf principle : If a facet A and another facet B belonging to the same subject are not to be separated though they are distinct from each other and thus separable, A and B should be kept together in the same round, even as a milch Cow and its unweaned calf are not separately sold out though they are distinct entities and, but are kept together in possession of the same owner (Prolegomena Pg. 427).

Ex "Enforcement of the function of the president of India"

The sequence will be India – President – Function – Enforcement

India, president, function are three facet but are not to be separated and can not put in different rounds.

Actand – Action – Actor – Tool Principle

In this principle there for four facet relate to each other. "If in a subject, facet B denotes action on facet A by facet C with facet D as a tool then the four facet should be arranged in the sequence A, B, CD, Ex Charkha. Cotton Spinning by Girls

Charkha	–	tool
Girls	–	Actor
Spinning	–	Action
Cotton	–	Actual

So facet sequence will be cotton, spinning, Girls, Charkha

Strings Indexing : Strings can be a phrase, a group of phrases, or a statement all specifically prepared for representing a document ex "user of World Wide Web for distributed learning in higher education" is an example of such strings. It has two characteristic.

1. Manually create a string to summarize the theme of a document
2. Mechanically generate index entries based on a given string for representation purpose

PRECIS and NEPHIS (Nested Phrase Indexting) are two example of string indexing.

Fuzzy searching : Fuzzy searching is designed to find terms that are spelled incorrectly at data entry or query input for e.g. The sequence secerence, secuance etc.

Cranfield I : Cranfield I was designed to test the comparative efficiency of four indexing systems on retrieval performance in an environment involving many other elements like indexer document, and search question. Recall and precision were used to measure retrieval performance in this project. The four indexing systems related for it are given below.

1. Universal decimal classification.
2. An Alphabetical subject catalogue.
3. A faceted classification scheme

4. A uniterm system of coordinate indexing

After a long process of test the finding were.

1. Uniterm system gave best recall.
2. It also disclosed the increased time in indexing which increased the level of recall also.

Cranfield II : Cranfield II was designed to know the effect of different indexing devices on retrieval performance . Indexing devices are synonyms, generic coordination, links and roles.

After a long process of test the finding were:

1. Single term indexing language were superior to any other type.
2. When concepts were used for indexing the performance can not be say good.
3. When controlled terms used with. BT and NT Its performance was not good response.

Automated and Automatic Indexing

All the activities involved in indexing can be put into two groups. Intellectual and mechanical.

Intellectual : The work of conceptual analysis and translation of the document to be indexed comes under the category of intellectual part of indexing.

Mechanical : Mechanical work of indexing lies in their alphabetisation and formatting of index entries.

Automated Indexing : When computers are used only to handle mechanical operation of indexing and intellectual portion is done by human being (indexer) it is called automated indexing.

Automatic Indexing : If the computer is used to handle both mechanical and intellectual portion of indexing it is called automatic indexing.

Proximity Searching : Proximity searching, allows the user to specify precisely the proximity or distance between two search terms and their relative location by using 'WITH' and 'NEAR' operator. A search statement 'information WITH technology' indicate that document must retrieve that have phrase 'information technology'

The extension of 'WITH' operation will be as eg. Information 2 with Technology retrieved documents as 'Information and Technology' 'Information and Networking' means 2 times information is used in two different documents.

Similarly we can use 'NEAR' operator eg. 'Information NEAR Technology, would produce documents either on information technology or technology information.

The n NEAR operator requires that terms linked by the operator be within n (n=1, 2...n) word of each other but in any order eg. Information 2 near technology result would be:

1. Information and technology
2. Information and network technology
3. Technology and information
4. Technology and business information

TCP/IP

TCP/IP is a five layer architecture. The five layers are

1. Application Layer
2. Transportation layer
3. Network layer a
4. Data link layer
5. Physical layer

Physical layer : The physical layer convents the data into a stream of bits which are then transferred on the available transmission medium.

Data link layer : The data link layer converts the

data into frames and transport them from one node to another node.

Network layer : The network layer in TCP/IP model is also known as the internet layer. It is responsible for delivering the data packets from the source to destination. At the network layer TCP/IP has defined IP protocol.

ARP

RARP

ICMP

IGMP

Transport Layer : The Transport layer transport the packet from source to destination computer TCP/IP defines TCP and UDP protocol at this level.

Application Layer : TCP/IP supports many applications like e-mail and file transfer. The application layer accept the data from the user and transfer it across the network.

UBUNTU (Operating system)

Ubuntu is a debian based Linux operating system. It is free software and named after the Southern African Philosophy which means "Humanity towards others" Ubuntu is collection of free softwares. Free software provides the freedom to edit & modify and distribute it. Ubuntu comes with installation in a wide range of software as Firefox, Libre office and computer games as Sudoku and Chess. Installation of Ubuntu is generally perfomed with live CD or live USB drive.

PHP : Now known as Hypertext pre processor PHP is a server side scripting language prepared for web environment but also used as general purpose programming language it was originally generated by Rasmus Lerdorf in 1995. But now produced by PHP Group.

PHP code is interpreted by web server with a PHP

processor module which generate the resulting web page. Previously it was known as personal home page.

EATPUT MODEL

The EATPUT model is designed by Dr. Anthory Debans in 1961 this model is used for analysing a information system. The model has been used in information science or system in a variety of areas.

The acronym EATPUT stands for:

1. Event
2. Acquisition
3. Transmission
4. Processing
5. Utilization
6. Transfer

Event : In this phase the system receives information in the form of image, digitally coded data, sound by another information system may be weather forecasting machine and event may be increase in humidity.

Acquisition : Acquisition phase is directly related to information sensors of an information system that sends data about the event phase.

Transmission : Transmission takes place between acquisition and processing phase. Water vapour sensors of the machine code information digitally and send it to next phase.

Processing : In processing phase data is stored, ordered, retrieved operated in order to form knowledge. The received knowledge is compare to last years, knowledge in case of water vapour example, and also measures under the meteorological principles in order to analyse the event of increasing humidity and may give result in % of humidity or its effect.

Utilization

In this phase the result obtained in processing phase interpret about the weather forecast in the form of rain and thunderstorm.

Transfer : The transfer phase is the action component of the system on the basis of information resulted from weather prediction machine to different phases process the public or resident of that area may be aware about the storm that may take place.

ISBN 13 digit : The ISBN 13 digit standard came into use from 1st January 2007 before it ISBN 10 digit was in use. ISBN 13 consists five groups as given below.

1. Prefix element
2. Registration group element
3. Registrant element
4. Publication element
5. Check digit

Prefix Element:

The first left side 3 digits is called prefix element. It is always 3 digits long. This element in effect makes are ISBN number into Universal Product Code known as an IAN (Before EAN). It is necessary as ISBN has an integration with product identification universally that is administrated by the EAN system. This prefix element is provided by GSI the global standard organisation a part of EAN interaction.

Ex. 978-81-7000 -665-7

978 is prefix element

Registration Group Element

This group of digit concern with geographical area or language of the book. It is one to 10 digits ISBN.

In our example 978-81-7000-665-7 ' 81' is registration group element.

Registrant Element

The registrant element is the 3 group in 13 digit ISBN. It indicate the identity of publisher within that Geographical area consist by Registration group element.In Ex. 978-81-7000-665-7, '7000 'is the registrant element.

Publication element

Publication element is given to that item (Book) that is published by registrant element with in geographical area consists by registration group Ex. 978-81-7000-665-7 '665' is the publication element digit.

Check digit

Check digit is used to check the validity of 13 digit ISBN in following way

978 81 7000 665

131 31 3131 313

(Each no is multiply by above digit)

9+21+8+24+1+21+0+0+0+18+6+15= 123

123 is divided by 10 = 12 and 3 is remainder now check digit 7 is added to remainder 3 = 10 so the ISBN is valid as 123+7 = 130 ¸ 10 = 13 and remainder 0 remainder = valid ISBN.

Webfeed : It is also as 'news feed'. It is a data format used to provide current update created in web-site to the end user who subscribes web feed of that web-site. This is done by the aggregator program (also called feed reader or news reader) running on users own machine. Through web server aggregater make a note for user on download item for him. Web feed in written in simple HTML that can by eaisly read by machine automatically.

Web feeds are operated by many news websites, weblogs and school. The two main web feed format are RSS and ATOM.

Web Portal

Web portal or public portal is a web-site or service that provide a number of resources and services such as e-mail forum, search engines and online shopping mall. The first web portal was on line services as AOL. After it excite , igoogle were introduced

IGoogle : igoogle is personal web portal launched by Google in May 2005 it was discontinued from 1st November 2013.

Semantic Web

Everyone is abreast with World Wide Web technology, that we can say traditional web technology. Semantic web are the server end client server technology that relate machine to machine conversation via www with the help of ontology or RDF. Ontology or RDF is used to capture the semantic relationship between two or more websites. In traditional web service the interoperability is in static and semantic meaning of message.

Ontology : Ontology are the structures framework for organizing information and it is used in artificial intelligence, semantic web software engineering etc.

According to Tom Gruber "An ontology is a description of the concept and relationship that can formally exist for an agent or a community of agent"

Z39.50

Z39.50 is an international standard client server application layer communication protocol used searching and retrieving information from a database using TCP/IP network. The standard of Z39.50 protocol is maintained by library of congress.

CODEN

The CODEN is designed by Charles Bishop. It is a memory aid for the publication in his reference collection bishop used four letters for coden system. This concept introduced in 1953 in his documentation system.

In 1961 Dr. Kuentzel at the 'American society for Testing of material introduced fifth character for CODEN. In 1976 (ASTM) American society standard defined six characters.

Today the first four character of the six character CODEN for a periodical are taken from the words of its title, followed by a fifth letter –one of the six letter (A-F) of the alphabet. The sixth and last character of the coden is an alphanumeric check character calculated from the preceeding letters. (CODEN Always use capital letters.)

International CODEN service located at chemical Abstract service .CAS beaome responsible for further development. CODEN is automatically developed to periodicals submitted to CAS.

Cloud Computing

Cloud computing, method of running application software and storing related data in central computer system and providing customers or other users access to them using internet. The customer need only web browser and operating software in their computer.

The term came in popular use in 2008 cloud computing provide 3 difference kinds of services.

SaaS : (Software as a Service) supply of discreate application to outside users.

HaaS (Hardware as a service) It is also called utility computing, grid computing, involves the provision of computer processing and data storage to out side users, who are able to run their own application and store their own data on remote system.

PaaS- (plateform as a service) – Involves the supply of remote computing, capacity along with a set of software development tools for user by out side software programmers.

h-Index

It is a method to know the published work of a scientist and its impact in library world by measuring its citation is number of papers. In other words h-Index reflects the number of publication and the number of citation per publication of a scientist. It is prepared by Jorge E. Hirsch. It is also called Hirsch Index or Hirsch Number.

SCOPUS

SCOPUS is the largest bibliographic database of Abstract and citation of peer reviewed literature. It covers nearly 21000 titles from 5000 publishers SCOPUS include the field of science, technology, medicine, social science art and humanities. It is a boon for research scholars of the world to know the status of research in their field. It is produce by Elsevier Academic publishing. It is available on line by subscription, Elsevier head Quarter is at Amsterdam.

Web of Science

It is a scientific Indexing service. It is maintained by Thomson Reuters of USA. It is online subscription based service provided to various institutions. It covers information from 1900 to present time. It provides the facility of depth search in a scientific discipline by accessing to multiple databases.

Information Literacy

Information Literacy means a sense to search, find retrieve and analyze information according to need. A student or user cannot learn everything in their field of study .Information literacy help him to in creating critical skill so that they can search pertinent information from huge store of knowledge. According to American library Association presidential committee on information literacy. " Ultimately information literate people are there who have learn how to learn. They know how to learn because they know how knowledge is organized how to find information and how to use information in such a way that others can learn from them. They are the people prepared for lifelong learning because they can always find the information needed for any task or decision at hand.

Data Smog

This term is coined by David Shenk. Data is used of information and literary meaning of smog is fog or haze worse by other pollutants in the atmosphere as smoke.

Now day's data smog is produced by large amount of information. Sometimes user confused that he made decision without searching all information that he/she needed or can consult. Information Literacy helps in preventing the problem of data smog.

11

UGC-NET Previous Years Question Paper with Solution

June 2012

LIBRARY AND INFORMATION SCIENCE

Paper – II

(1) Who was the Chairman of 'National Policy on Library & Information Systems' (1986)?

(a) D.N. Banerjee (b) D.P. Chattopadhyay

(c) Sam Pitroda (d) Kalpana Dasgupta

(2) The significance of the year 2011 for LIS education in India is

(a) Golden Jubilee year

(b) Platinum Jubilee year

(c) Diamond Jubilee year

(d) Centenary year

(3) Digital Reference Service can be offered through

(a) FAX (b) OPAC

(c) Ask your librarian (d) Consortia

(4) "Biotechnology" is formed as a result of

(a) Fusion (b) Lamination

(c) Fission (d) Agglomeration

(5) The order of significance of "Thing, Material and Action" among various components of a compound subject was expanded by

(a) J. Kaiser
(b) E.J. Coates
(c) J.R. Sharp
(d) J.E.L. Farradane

(6) Relational Database is

(a) A work which has some relationship to another work
(b) A symbol representing relationship between two concepts
(c) Manipulation commands which relate records in different fields
(d) All of the above

(7) "Shodhganga" is a repository of

(a) E-Resources
(b) E-Thesis
(c) E-Journals
(d) E-Books

(8) Which of the following tests can be employed for hypothesis testing?

(a) F-test
(b) Chi-square test
(c) t-test
(d) All of the above

(9) 'RRRLF' falls under the:

(a) Ministry of Human Resource Development
(b) Ministry of Information & Broadcasting
(c) Ministry of Culture
(d) Ministry of Science & Technology

(10) "Internet Public Library" is being maintained by

(a) MIT, Massachusettes
(b) University of Michigan
(c) University of Arizona
(d) Dresal University

(11) What are the major driving forces behind an 'Information society'?

(i) RTI (ii) I.C.T.
(iii) Internet (iv) I.T. ACT

Codes:

(A) (ii) & (i) are correct
(B) (ii) and (iv) are correct
(C) (i) and (iv) are correct
(D) (ii) and (iii) are correct

(12) Which libraries are functioning as depository libraries?

(i) Delhi Public Library
(ii) Connemara Public Library
(iii) British Council Library
(iv) Central Reference Library

Codes:

(A) (i), (iii) and (iv) are correct
(B) (i) and (iii) are correct
(C) (i) and (ii) are correct
(D) (ii) and (iii) are correct

(13) Which of the following are 'Inclusive geographical sources'

(i) Maps (ii) Atlases
(iii) Encyclopaedias (iv) Yearbooks

Codes:

(A) (i) & (ii) are correct (B) (iii) & (iv) are correct
(C) (ii) & (iii) are correct (D) (ii) & (iv) are correct

(14) Which principles are corollary to Wall- picture principle?

(i) Cow-calf principle
(ii) Principle of later-in-time
(iii) Whole-organ principle
(iv) All of the above

Codes:

(A) (i) and (ii) are correct

(B) (ii) and (iii) are correct

(C) (i) and (iii) are correct

(D) (i) and (iv) are correct

(15) The factors that influence computer file organisation are

(i) Speed of access (ii) Storage space

(iii) Fixed length fields (iv) File volatility

Codes:

(A) (i), (ii) and (iii) are correct

(B) (i), (ii) and (iv) are correct

(C) (ii), (iii) and (iv) are correct

(D) (i) (iii) and (iv) are correct

(16) Major problems of 'Information Communication Technology' are

(i) Information overload

(ii) Information insecurity

(iii) Lack of innovative technologies

(iv) Lack of control over communication

Codes:

(A) (ii) and (iv) are correct

(B) (i) and (iv) are correct

(C) (i), (ii) and (iv) are correct

(D) (i), (ii) and (iii) are correct

(17) Which of the following are 'Open Source Content Management System'?

(i) Drupal (ii) Atex

(iii) Joomla (iv) Open Cms

Codes:

(A) (i) (ii) and (iv) are correct

(B) (i) (ii) and (iii) are correct

(C) (ii) (iii) and (iv) are correct

(D) (i) (iii) and (iv) are correct

(18) Which of the following are not styles of citation?

(i) Anglo American Cataloguing Rules

(ii) MLA handbook for Writers of Research Papers

(iii) Chicago Manual of Style

(iv) Little Science Big Science

Codes:

(A) (i) and (ii) are correct

(B) (iii) and (iv) are correct

(C) (i) and (iv) are correct

(D) (ii) and (iii) are correct

(19) Which of the following are Schools of Management thought?

(i) Scientific Management School

(ii) Human Behavioural School

(iii) Classical School

(iv) School of Authority

Codes:

(A) (ii) and (iv) are correct

(B) (i) (ii) and (iv) are correct

(C) (iii) and (iv) are correct

(D) (i) (ii) and (iii) are correct

(20) **Assertion (A) :** Users can have access to large number of e-journals.

Reason (R) : Users are not aware of using e-journals.

Codes:

(A) (A) is true, but (R) is false

(B) Both (A) and (R) are true, but (R) is not the correct explanation of (A)

(C) (A) is false, (R) is true

(D) Both (A) and ® are true and (R) is the correct explanation of (A)

(21) **Assertion (A) :** Book selection must be done judiciously.

Reason (R) : Resource sharing is the need of the hour.

Codes:

(A) Both (A) and (R) are true, but (R) is not the correct explanation of (A)

(B) (A) is false, (R) is true

(C) (A) is true, (R) is false

(D) Both (A) and (R) are false

(22) **Assertion (A) :** Primary sources provide most authentic information for research.

Reason (R) : Primary sources are highly unorganised

Codes:

(A) (A) is false, (R) is true

(B) (A) is true, (R) is false

(C) Both (A) and (R) is correct and (R) is the correct explanation of (A)

(D) Both (A) and (R) is correct and (R) is not the correct explanation of (A)

(23) **Assertion (A) :** Abstracting services facilitate literature review.

Reason (R) : Literature review summarises major finding of various studies.

Codes:

(A) (A) is true, (R) is false

(B) Both (A) and (R)true and (R) is the correct explanation of (A)

(C) (A) is false, (R) is true

(D) Both (A) and (R) is correct and (R) is not the correct explanation of (A)

(24) **Assertion (A) :** 'Name Authority File" should be used in a library.

Reason (R) : All works of an author should be collocated.

Codes:

(A) (A) is true, (R) is false

(B) Both (A) and (R)true and (R) is the correct explanation of (A)

(C) (A) is false, (R) is true

(D) Both (A) and (R) is correct and (R) is not the correct explanation of (A)

(25) **Assertion (A) :** Classification plays a significant role in online retrieval.

Reason (R) : Classification played an important role in manual system.

Codes:

(A) (A) is true, but (R) is false

(B) (A) and (R) are false

(C) Both (A) and (R) is true

(D) (A) is false, (R) is true

(26) **Assertion (A) :** If changes cannot be adopted to its framework, the organisational equilibrium will be imbalanced.

Reason (R) : Organisation works in an environment which is marked by dynamic characteristics

Codes:

(A) (A) is true, but (R) is false

(B) (A) is false, but (R) is true

(C) Both (A) and (R) true

(D) Both (A) and (R)false

(27) **Assertion (A)** : There is need to continuous evaluation and appreciation of value of libraries.

Reason (R) : There is economic pressure on public budget.

Codes:

(A) Both (A) and (R) true

(B) Both (A) and (R) are false

(C) (A) is true, but (R) is false

(D) (A) is false, but (R) is true

(28) **Assertion (A)** : System analysis identifies the flow of work.

Reason (R) : System analysis is not necessary if the library is automated.

Codes:

(A) (A) is false, but (R) is true

(B) (A) is true, but (R) is false

(C) Both (A) and (R) are false

(D) Both (A) and (R)true

(29) Arrange the following associations according to their year of establishment:

(i) IASLIC (ii) ASLIB

(iii) ALA (iv) SLA

Codes:

(A) (B)

(C) (D)

(30) Arrange the following according to their year of enactment in India:

(i) Freedom of Information Act

(ii) Right to Information Act

(iii) Copyright Act (Revised)

(iv) Information Technology Act

Codes :

(A) (iv), (ii), (i) , (iii) (B) (iii), (iv), (i) (ii),

(C) (ii), (iii), (iv), (i) (D) (i), (iv), (ii), (iii)

(31) Arrange the following publications according to their year of origin.

(i) Social Science Citation Index

(ii) LISA

(iii) Library Literature and Information Science

(iv) Library Journal

Codes:

(A) (i), (iii), (iv), (ii) (B) (ii), (i), (iii), (iv)

(C) (iv), (iii), (ii), (i) (D) (iii), (ii), (iv), (i)

(32) Arrange the following according to their year of origin:

(i) Broad System of Ordering

(ii) Classification in Online Systems

(iii) Automated Keyword Classification

(iv) Classification Research Group

Codes:

(A) (iv), (iii), (i), (ii) (B) (i), (ii), (iv) (iii),

(C) (iii), (i) (ii), (iv), (D) (ii), (iv), (iii), (i)

(33) Arrange the following according to their year of origin:

(i) Bradford;s Law

(ii) Lotka's Law

(iii) Statistical Bibliography

(iv) Zipf's Law

Codes:

(A) (i), (iii), (iv), (ii) (B) (i), (ii), (iv) (iii),

(C) (iv), (iii), (i), (ii) (D) (iii), (ii), (iv), (i)

(34) "Prevention of Cholera in India" generates following index terms according to modified 'Chain Indexing', arrange them in correct order

(i) India (ii) Cholera
(iii) Disease (iv) Treatment
(v) Medicine

Codes:

(A) (iii), (iv), (i), (ii), (v) (B) (ii), (i), (iii), (iv), (v)
(C) (iv), (iii), (ii), (v) (i) (D) (i) (iii), (iv), (v) (ii),

(35) Arrange the following according to their year of first publication:

(i) Encyclopaedia Britannica
(ii) Encyclopaedia Americana
(iii) Encyclopaedia of Library and Information Science
(iv) McGraw-Hill Encyclopaedia of Science and Technology

Codes:

(A) (iv), (iii), (i), (ii) (B) (i), (ii), (iv), (iii)
(C) (iii), (i), (iv), (ii) (D) (ii), (iv), (i), (iii)

(36) Arrange the following according to their year of establishment:

(i) NIC (ii) DESIDOC
(iii) NISCAIR (iv) NASSDOC

Codes:

(A) (i), (iii), (ii), (iv) (B) (iii), (i), (iv), (ii)
(C) (iv), (i), (iii), (ii) (D) (ii), (iv), (i), (iii)

(37) Arrange the following public library Acts according to their year of enactment:

(i) Uttar Pradesh PL Act
(ii) Arunanchal Pradesh PL Act
(iii) Orissa PL Act

(iv) Gujarat PL Act

Codes:

(A) (iv), (iii), (i), (ii) (B) (ii), (iii), (i), (iv)

(C) (ii), (i), (iv), (iii) (D) (iii), (ii), (i), (iv),

(38) Match the following:

	List – I	**List – II**
(a)	Obligation of the State	(i) First Law
(b)	Shelf Arrangement & Catalogue	(ii) Second Law
(c)	Open Access & Shalf Arrangement	(iii) Third Law
(d)	Library location/ hours	(iv) Fourth

Codes :	**(a)**	**(b)**	**(c)**	**(d)**
(A)	ii	iv	iii	i
(B)	iv	iii	iii	i
(C)	i	iii	iv	ii
(D)	iii	ii	i	iv

(39) Match the following:

	List – I	**List – II**
(a)	Asian Recorder	(i) Location of specific volume of journal
(b)	Union Catalogue of Scientific Serials	(ii) Articles on Green Revolution
(c)	Books-in-Print	(iii) Obituary of Dev-Anand
(d)	Social Science Index	(iv) Availability of books

Codes :	**(a)**	**(b)**	**(c)**	**(d)**
(A)	iv	iii	i	ii
(B)	i	iv	ii	iii
(C)	iii	i	iv	ii
(D)	ii	iv	iii	i

(40) Match the following:

	List – I		List – II
(a)	User orientation	(i)	Bibliographic service
(b)	Information repackaging	(ii)	Reference service
(c)	Translation	(iii)	Digest service
(d)	Indexing	(iv)	Support service

Codes :	**(a)**	**(b)**	**(c)**	**(d)**
(A)	i	iv	iii	ii
(B)	iii	ii	i	iv
(C)	iv	i	ii	iii
(D)	ii	iii	iv	i

(41) Match the following :

	List – I		List – II
(a)	Textual representation	(i)	Pascal
(b)	Computer language	(ii)	Gopher
(c)	Network tool	(iii)	Boolean operators
(d)	Searching technique	(iv)	ASCII

Codes :	**(a)**	**(b)**	**(c)**	**(d)**
(A)	iv	i	ii	iii
(B)	i	iv	iii	ii
(C)	iii	ii	iv	i
(D)	ii	iv	iii	i

(42) Match the following :

	List – I		List – II
(a)	Law of Parsimony	(i)	Classification
(b)	Principle of Osmosis	(ii)	F.W. Lancaster
(c)	Paperless Society	(iii)	Overall Economy
(d)	APUPA pattern	(iv)	Re-classification

Codes :	**(a)**	**(b)**	**(c)**	**(d)**
(A)	ii	i	iv	iii
(B)	iv	ii	i	iii
(C)	iii	iv	ii	i
(D)	i	iii	ii	iv

(43) Match the following

List – I	**List – II**
(a) Hubs	(i) A physical layer device used to interconnect the media of segments of an extended network
(b) Repeater	(ii) A physical layer device that connects multiple computers each via a dedicated cable
(c) Bus Topology	(iii) Multiple bridges known for transfer of data between different parts
(d) Switches	(iv) A straight line data highway that carries network information from one network station to another

Codes :	**(a)**	**(b)**	**(c)**	**(d)**
(A)	iii	iv	ii	i
(B)	ii	i	iv	iii
(C)	iv	i	iii	ii
(D)	i	iii	ii	iv

(44) Match the following :

List – I	**List – II**
(a) RRRLF	(i) Delhi
(b) Connemara Public Library	(ii) Patna
(c) NISCAIR	(iii) Kolkara
(d) Khuda Baksh	(iv) Chennai

Codes :	(a)	(b)	(c)	(d)
(A)	iv	iii	ii	i
(B)	ii	iii	iv	i
(C)	iii	iv	i	ii
(D)	iv	i	ii	iii

(45) Match the following :

List – I	List – II
(a) Right man at right library	(i) Annual financial statement
(b) Budget	(ii) Deployment
(c) Journal	(iii) TQM
(d) Identifying user's views and expectations	(iv) ISSN

Codes :	(a)	(b)	(c)	(d)
(A)	iii	i	ii	iv
(B)	ii	i	iv	iii
(C)	iv	ii	iii	i
(D)	i	iii	iv	ii

(46) Why digital objects become inaccessible quickly?

(a) Because of unforeseen advancement of technology

(b) It is independent of human intervention

(c) It is independent of any technological advancement

(d) None of the above

(47) Reinterpretation is a digital preservation strategy where curator intends to

(a) Upgrade file formats

(b) Upgrade stroge mechanism

(c) Recreate a work

(d) Upgrade operating system

(48) What is the focus of system emulation?

(a) Developing systems that mimic hardware

(b) Developing systems that mimic software

(c) Developing systems that mimic file formats

(d) None of the above

(49) Which of the following is true about migration preservation strategy?

(a) Migration is not related to the viewing problem

(b) Migration is related to the viewing problem

(c) Migration requires comprehensive documentation

(d) Migration does not have a technical origin

(50) Refreshing preservation strategy focuses on

(a) Comprehensive documentation of original artefact

(b) Development of operating system

(c) Not on viewing problem

(d) Upgradation of storage mechanism

ANSWERS

01 (b)	02 (d)	03 (c)	04 (a)
05 (b)	06 (c)	07 (b)	08 (d)
09 (c)	10 (d)	11 (d)	12 (c)
13 (b)	14 (c)	15 (b)	16 (c)
17 (d)	18 (c)	19 (d)	20 (b)
21 (a)	22 (d)	23 (c)	24 (b)
25 (d)	26 (c)	27 (a)	28 (b)
29 (c)	30 (b)	31 (c)	32 (a)
33 (d)	34 (c)	35 (b)	36 (d)
37 (a)	38 (a)	39 (c)	40 (d)
41 (a)	42 (c)	43 (b)	44 (c)
45 (b)	46 (a)	47 (c)	48 (a)
49 (b)	50 (d)		

June 2012

LIBRARY AND INFORMATION SCIENCE

Paper – III

(1) The initiation, selection, exploration, formulation, collection and presentation are two stages of which model of information seeking behaviur

(a) Ellis Model (b) Krikelas Model

(c) Kuhlthou Model (d) Vilson Model

(2) Jubilee Project is associated with what

(a) Evaluation of electronic information services

(b) Public library survey

(c) Strategic management of libraries

(d) Scale development

(3) The publisher of "Information Power: Building Partnership for Learning" is

(a) AASL (b) AECT

(c) ALA (d) ILA

(4) In 1974, Zurkowski used for the first time which of the following term?

(a) Digital Literacy (b) Media Literacy

(c) Computer Literacy (d) Information Literacy

(5) Inference Engine is a part of which information system?

(a) Management information system

(b) Decision Support System

(c) Expert System

(d) Open System

(6) Which of the following is not related to case study approach in a research design?

(a) Indepth Study

(b) Study of one/limited cases

(c) General study

(d) Little concern about generalisation to a large population

(7) "Students' visit to Library is influenced by the availability of Internet". State "Students' visit to library" is which kind of variable?

(a) Independent Variable

(b) Intervening Variable

(c) Dependent Variable

(d) Intercept Variable

(8) Idiographic hypothesis is directed towards predicting the behaviour of

(a) An Individual

(b) Group of People

(c) Messes

(d) People from same school of thought

(9) In the process of reasoning when we start with a specific statement, and conclude to a general statement, it is called

(a) Deductive Reasoning

(b) Inductive Reasoning

(c) Abnormal Reasoning

(d) Transcendental Reasoning

(10) Solomon Four group design is related to

(a) Field studies

(b) Pretest-post test control group design

(c) Data Analysis Model

(d) Statistical Technique

(11) The information network that connects Universities and Colleges in United Kingdom:

(a) JANET (b) SERCNET

(c) OCLC (d) BONET

(12) Internet filtering is

(a) A form of censorship

(b) Acceptable user policy

(c) Access to inappropriate material

(d) Blocking internet facility

(13) Which one of the following is a Bulletin Board Service on Internet?

(a) Picaso (b) Google talk

(c) Blog (d) Oovoo

(14) Virus is a software which can

(a) Manipulate data (b) Replicate itself

(c) Damage computer (d) All the above

(15) Which one of the following protocol is used in file transfer over internet?

(a) FTP (b) SMTP

(c) POP (d) TCP/IP

(16) Scaler chain shows

(a) Authority structure

(b) Scale of performance of staff

(c) Chain for locating racks

(d) A link in the chain

(17) Blair and Maron evaluation study on retrieval effectiveness of full text search is called

(a) SMART Retrieval Experiment

(b) MEDLARS evaluation study

(c) STAIRS project

(d) Cranefield – II Project

(18) In cataloguing, the square brackets [ ] are used

(a) To enclose information taken from outside

(b) To enclose the details of printed/manufacturer

(c) To enclose series statements

(d) To enclose statement of accompanying material

(19) Which Section of AACR – II (R) deals with serial publications?

(a) Part – A, Section – 3

(b) Part – B, Section – 3

(c) Part – A, Section – 12

(d) Part – B, Section – 12

(20) When two or more basic subjects having same relational approach form a specific subject, the relation is termed as

(a) Speciater relation (b) Co-ordinate relation

(c) Phase relation (d) Hierarchical relation

(21) The concept of 'Stopword' list is relevant in the context of

(a) Uniform Indexing (b) Citation Indexing

(c) Chain Indexing (d) Keyword Indexing

(22) A version of KWIC augmented with author/name is called

(a) WADEX (b) KWOC

(c) KWAC (d) KWIC

(23) 'Segmentation' is associated with

(A) Reference Service (B) Market Survey Report

(C) Digest Service (D) Indexing Service

(24) State of the art report generally highlights

(A) General Aspects

(B) Technical Aspects

(C) Administrative Aspects

(D) All of the above

(25) Who propounded "Minimum, Middling and Maximum Theories" of reference service?

(A) C.M. Winchell (B) James I. Wyer

(C) Samuel Rothstein (D) D.W. Lewis.

(26) Even though 'Xerography' is a photocopying method, but it is called

(A) Diazographic (B) Thermographic

(C) Electrofax (D) Electrostatic

(27) 'CODEN' is connected with

(A) Books (B) Serials

(C) Reports (D) Gray Literature

(28) Roget's International Thesaurus is a

(A) Classified List of Words

(B) Book of Synonyms

(C) List of Standard Terms

(D) List of Scientific Terms

(29) Information about scale and projection can be found in

(A) Encyclopaedias

(B) Hand books of Manuals

(C) Geographical sources

(D) Directories

(30) Who of the following is not the author of any referencc book?

(A) C.M. Winchell (B) William A Katz

(C) Louis Shores (D) Maurice B. Line

(31) Identify the odd one out.

(A) ANSI (B) BIS

(C) BSI (D) ESPN

(32) Which of the following is not a part of word treatment in language dictionaries?

(A) Gloss

(B) Vernacular

(C) Etymology

(D) Grammatical information

(33) Where the first M. Phil programme in Library and Information Science was started in India?

(A) University of Madras (B) University of Delhi

(C) University of Mysore (D) University of Bombay

(34) Corollary for Second Law of Library Science is

(A) Books for all (B) Free Books Service

(C) Free Library Service (D) Books every where

(35) Which of the following is not the prerequisite for a National Information Policy?

(A) Legislative Frame work

(B) Production of national bibliography

(C) Advisory and Aministrative body

(D) ICT infrastructure facilities

(36) World Intellectual Property Organization is related to

(A) UNESCO

(B) United Nations

(C) U.S. Organization

(D) International Law Organization

(37) Redundancy of information is

(A) Unnecessary and should be eliminated

(B) Unnecessary but cannot be avoided

(C) Necessary and some times useful

(D) Necessary and always desirable

(38) Which source would you consult to know the "Impact Factor" of Journal publications?

(i) Web of Science (ii) Science Direct

(iii) ESOPUS (iv) EBSCO

Codes:

(A) (i) and (iv) (B) (ii) and (iii)

(C) (i) and (iii) (D) (iii) and (iv)

(39) Research is conducted to:

(i) Generate new knowledge

(ii) Develop a theory

(iii) Develop communication skills

(iv) Re-interpret existing knowledge

Codes:

(A) (i), (iii) and (ii) are cprrect

(B) (iii), (ii) and (i) are correct

(C) (i), (ii) and (iv) are correct

(D) (i), (iii) and (iv) are correct

(40) Radio Frequency Identification is used in library for:

(i) Circulation of Documents

(ii) Cataloguing of Documents

(iii) Security of Documents

(iv) Acquisition of Documents

Codes:

(A) (i) and (ii) are correct.

(B) (ii) and (iv) are correct.

(C) (iii) and (ii) are correct.

(D) (i) and (iii) arc correct.

(41) BIOS contains:

(i) Operating System Program

(ii) Bootstrap Program

(iii) Application System program

(iv) Convert Character to Code program

Codes :

(A) (i) and (ii) are correct

(B) (ii) and (iii) are correct

(C) (iii) and (iv) are correct

(D) (ii) and (iv) are correct

(42) Science Citation Index is published by

(A) Thomson Reuters (B) H.W. Wilson

(C) Whitaker (D) R.R. Bowker

(43) In the information transfer cycles, internet is acting as

(i) Primary Publisher (ii) Secondary Publisher

(iii) Tertiary Publisher (iv) Primary Distributor

Codes:

(A) (i), (iii) and (iv) are correct

(B) (i) (ii) and (iv) are correct

(C) (ii) (iii) and (iv) are correct

(D) (i) (ii) and (iii) are correct

(44) Methods and Techniques of Human Resource Planning includes

(i) Selection and Recruitment

(ii) Induction and Placement

(iii) Quality Management

(iv) Performance Evaluation

Codes:

(A) (i), (iv) and (ii) are correct

(B) (iv) (iii) and (i) are correct

(C) (i), (ii) and (iv) are correct

(D) (iii) and (i) are correct

(45) **Assertion (A)** : Netiquette mandates that you do your best to act within the laws of cyberspace and society.

Reason (R) : Railing to respect other people's privacy is bad Netiquette.

(A) Both (A) and (R) are false

(B) Both (A) and (R) are true

(C) (A) is true, but (R) is false

(D) (A) is false, but (R) is true

(46) **Assertion (A) :** Modern Integrated Library Management Softwares other user friendly Graphical User Interfaces (GUI) on the web.

Reason (R) : Almost every module of modern Integrated Library Management Software is accessible through the internet

Codes:

(A) Both (A) and (R) are correct.

(B) (A) is correct but (R) is wrong.

(C) Both (A) and (R) are wrong.

(D) (A) is wrong but (R) is correct.

(47) **Assertion (A) :** Open System Interconnection allows connectivity of ICT components.

Reason (R) : Network Printer goes slow if it is OSI compatible.

Codes:

(A) Both (A) and (R) are true.

(B) Both (A) and (R) are false.

(C) (A) is false but (R) is true

(D) (A) is true but (R) is false.

(48) **Assertion (A) :** Many libraries have no written collection development policyand yet have sound collection.

Reason (R) : Demand driven collection plays a strong role in having a soundcollection

Codes:

(A) (A) is true and (R) is false.

(B) (A) is false and (R) is true.

(C) Both (A) and (R) are true.

(D) Both (A) & (R) are false.

(49) **Assertion (A) :** Browne charging system is simple and less time consuming.

Reason (R) : There is permanent issue record available.

Codes:

(A) (A) is false but (R) is true.

(B) (A) is true but (R) is false.

(C) (A) is true and (R) is partially true.

(D) Both (A) & (R) are false

(50) **Assertion (A) :** Collection of audio materials is less used in Academic Libraries.

Reason (R) : People consider these materials intellectually less sound and fit only for recreation purpose.

Codes:

(A) (A) is false but (R) is true.

(B) (A) is true but (R) is false.

(C) Both (A) & (R) are true

(D) Both (A) & (R) are false

(51) **Assertion (A) :** Introduction of TQM in libraries is not possible.

Reason (R) : It requires open, cooperative culture and employees responsiveness for customer satisfaction.

Codes:

(A) Both (A) & (R) are true.

(B) (A) is true, (R) is false.

(C) (A) is false, (R) is true.

(D) Both (A) & (R) are false.

(52) **Assertion (A) :** An indexing language is an artificial language and it used controlled vocabulary.

Reason (R) : Controlled vocabulary provides relation between and among terms.

Codes:

(A) Both (A) & (R) are true.

(B) (A) is frue, (R) is false.

(C) (A) is false but (R) are true.

(D) Both (A) & (R) are false.

(53) **Assertion (A) :** Marketing of Information products is the need of the day.

Reason (R) : Information is a resource which consumes lot of time and money.

Codes:

(A) (A) is true but (R) is false.

(B) (A) is false but (R) is true.

(C) Both (A) and (R) are true.

(D) Both (A) and (R) are false.

(54) **Assertion (A) :** Colan classification is an enumerative classification scheme.

Reason (R) : Colon classification has adopted analytics-synthetic approach for the construction of class number

Codes:

(A) (A) is true but (R) is false.

(B) (A) is false but (R) is true.

(C) Both (A) and (R) are true.

(D) Both (A) and (R) are false.

(55) **Assertion (A) :** INFLIBNET provides document delivery service to all types of libraries in India

Reason (R) : Modern technologies made it possible for electronic transmission of required documents.

Codes:

(A) Both (A) and (R) are correct.

(B) (A) is wrong but (R)is correct.

(C) Both (A) and (R) are wrong

(D) (A) is correct but (R) is wrong.

(56) **Assertion (A) :** LIS Education in India achieved a landmark of 100 years but quality is compromised.

Reason (R) : Unplanned proliferation of LIS schools and open learning programmes

Codes:

(A) Both (A) and (R) are true.

(B) Both (A) and (R) are false.

(C) (A) is false but (R) is true.

(D) (A) is true but (R) is false.

(57) **Assertion (A) :** LIS education is not uniform throughout India.

Reason (R) : Adoption of UGC model syllabus is not mandatory, Local LIS requirements varies.

Codes:

(A) (A) is true but (R) is false.

(B) (A) is false but (R) is true.

(C) Both (A) and (R) are true.

(D) Both (A) and (R) are false.

(58) **Assertion (A) :** There is need for Library Legislation in all States of India.

Reason (R) : To make public Library System independent and without political influence.

Codes:

(A) Both (A) & (R) are true.

(B) (A) is true but (R) is false

(C) Both (A) & (R) are false

(D) (A) is false but (R) is true.

(59) **Assertion (A) :** Thought information is considered as a commodity, Libraries are not sound in finances.

Reason (R) : All types of Libraries have failed in promoting information as a commodity

(i) (A) is true but (R) is false

(ii) (A) is false but (R) is true.

(iii) Both (A) & (R) are true.

(iv) Both (A) & (R) are false

(60) What is the correct order of SCONUL's "Seven Pillar Model of Information Skills" ?

List – I	**List – II**
(a) Konnemara Public Library	(i) Patna
(b) Khudabaksha Oriental Public Library	(ii) Kolkata
(c) Asiatic Society Library	(iii) Chennai
(d) National Library	(iv) Mumbai

Codes :	**(a)**	**(b)**	**(c)**	**(d)**
(A)	iv	ii	I	iii
(B)	iv	I	ii	iii
(C)	iii	ii	I	iv
(D)	iii	I	iv	ii

(61) Match the following:

List – I	**List – II**
(a) Ibid	(i) See
(b) Loc.cit	(ii) Previously cites
(c) Op.cit	(iii) Same reference cited immediately above
(d) Vide	(iv) The same place cited

Codes :	**(a)**	**(b)**	**(c)**	**(d)**
(A)	i	ii	iii	iv
(B)	ii	I	iv	iii
(C)	iii	iv	ii	i
(D)	iv	iii	i	ii

(62) Match the following:

	List – I	List – II
(a)	Cole and Eales	(i) Statistical Bibliography
(b)	Hume	(ii) Scientometrics
(c)	Pritchard	(iii) Statistical Analysis
(d)	T. Braun	(iv) Bibliometrics

Codes :	(a)	(b)	(c)	(d)
(A)	iv	iii	ii	i
(B)	iii	i	iv	ii
(C)	ii	iii	i	iv
(D)	i	iii	iv	ii

(63) Match the following:

	List – I	List – II
(a)	Thurston scale	(i) Sharing individual preference in a group
(b)	Semantic Differential Scale	(ii) Group of Judges
(c)	Likert scale	(iii) Selection from two opposite position
(d)	Sociometric scale	(iv) Intensity structure

Codes :	(a)	(b)	(c)	(d)
(A)	i	iv	ii	iii
(B)	ii	iii	iv	i
(C)	iv	i	iii	ii
(D)	iii	ii	iv	i

(64) Match the following :

	List – I	List – II
(a)	Vidyanidhi	(i) Institutional Repository
(b)	TKDL	(ii) Electronic Theses & Dissertations

(c) DOAJ (iii) Digital Library of Journals

(d) E-Prints @ IISc (iv) Digital Archive

Codes :	(a)	(b)	(c)	(d)
(A)	ii	iv	iii	i
(B)	iii	ii	i	iv
(C)	iv	iii	ii	i
(D)	i	ii	iv	iii

(65) Match the following :

List – I	List – II
(a) HTML File	(i) Text Format
(b) PDF File	(ii) Film Format
(c) JPG File	(iii) Web Format
(d) AVI File	(iv) Image Format

Codes :	(a)	(b)	(c)	(d)
(A)	i	ii	iv	iii
(B)	iii	i	iv	ii
(C)	i	iv	ii	iii
(D)	iv	iii	i	ii

(66) Match the following

List – I	List – II
(a) DRUPAL	(i) Integrated Library Management Software
(b) Moodle	(ii) Digital Library Software
(c) D space	(iii) Content Management Software
(d) New Gen Lib	(iv) Learning Management Software

Codes :	(a)	(b)	(c)	(d)
(A)	iv	iii	ii	i
(B)	ii	i	iv	iii
(C)	iii	iv	ii	i
(D)	i	ii	iii	iv

(67) Match the following :

	List – I	List – II
(a)	Face Book	(i) Video Networking site
(b)	Research Gate	(ii) Social Networking site
(c)	Oovoo	(iii) Academic Networking site
(d)	Ficker	(iv) Photo Networking site

Codes :	**(a)**	**(b)**	**(c)**	**(d)**
(A)	i	iii	ii	iv
(B)	iv	i	ii	iv
(C)	ii	iii	i	iv
(D)	iii	iv	i	ii

(68) Match the following :

	List – I	List – II
(a)	Small set of dependent activities that form longest path of activity network	(i) PERT
(b)	Delighting the customer by fully meeting their needs	(ii) CPM
(c)	Interconnecting networks depicting tasks, duration and dependency	(iii) Delphi
(d)	Making better forecasts, judgements and advice	(iv) TQM

Codes :	**(a)**	**(b)**	**(c)**	**(d)**
(A)	i	iii	ii	iv
(B)	ii	iv	i	iii
(C)	iii	iv	ii	i
(D)	iv	ii	i	iii

(69) Match the following :

	List – I	List – II
(a)	Transaction Processing	(i) Lower Level Managers

(b) Operational control (ii) Clerical Staff

(c) Management control (iii) Top Level Managers

(d) Strategic Planning (iv) Middle Level Managers

Codes :	**(a)**	**(b)**	**(c)**	**(d)**
(A)	iii	ii	iv	i
(B)	ii	i	iv	iii
(C)	iv	ii	iii	i
(D)	i	ii	iv	iii

(70) Match the following :

List – I	**List – II**
(a) Classical School	(i) John cotton Danna
(b) X & Y Theory	(ii) Henry Fayol
(c) Newark Charging System	(iii) Peter Drucker
(d) MBO	(iv) Douglas McGregor

Codes :	**(a)**	**(b)**	**(c)**	**(d)**
(A)	i	iii	iv	ii
(B)	iii	iv	i	ii
(C)	ii	iv	i	iii
(D)	iii	ii	iv	i

(71) Match the following :

List – I	**List – II**
(a) C.A. Catter	(i) Selective Listing
(b) Kaiser	(ii) Thing-part-material-action
(c) J.R. Sharp	(iii) Concrete and process
(d) D.J. Coates	(iv) Syndetic cataloguing

Codes :	**(a)**	**(b)**	**(c)**	**(d)**
(A)	iv	i	ii	iii
(B)	iv	iii	i	ii
(C)	iii	iv	ii	i
(D)	ii	iii	iv	i

(72) Match the following :

	List – I		List – II
(a)	Guidance to use RTI Act	(i)	Documentation service
(b)	Orientation in use of multimedia	(ii)	Referral service
(c)	Providing user with list of information sources	(iii)	Informative Literacy
(d)	Directing the user of INFLIBNET to seek needed information	(iv)	Reference service

Codes :	**(a)**	**(b)**	**(c)**	**(d)**
(A)	iii	ii	i	iv
(B)	iv	ii	iii	i
(C)	ii	i	iv	iii
(D)	iv	iii	i	ii

(73) Match the following :

	List – I		List – II
(a)	Whitaker's Almanack	(i)	Year of starting 'Publishers Weekly'
(b)	Ulrich's International Periodicals Directory	(ii)	Availability of V 50 of 'Library Journal'
(c)	National Union Catalogue of Scientific Serials in India	(iii)	Information on discontinuation of New Encyclopaedia Britanniaca
(d)	Data India	(iv)	Astronomical information

Codes :	**(a)**	**(b)**	**(c)**	**(d)**
(A)	iv	i	ii	iii
(B)	ii	iv	i	iii
(C)	iii	ii	i	iv
(D)	i	iv	ii	iii

(74) Match the following :

	List – I		**List – II**
(a)	J. Thompson	(i)	Basic Statistics for Libraries
(b)	S. Halkett of J Laing	(ii)	Planning of Academic and Research Buildings
(c)	William A Katz	(iii)	Dictionary of anonymous and pseudonymous literature
(d)	K.D. Metcalf	(iv)	Introduction to reference work

Codes :	**(a)**	**(b)**	**(c)**	**(d)**
(A)	i	ii	iv	iii
(B)	i	iii	iv	ii
(C)	ii	iv	i	iii
(D)	iv	ii	iii	i

(75) Match the following :

	List – I		**List – II**
(a)	Budget prepared using previous period budget	(i)	Formula Budget
(b)	Budget based on norms and standards	(ii)	Incremental Budget
(c)	Budget planned integrating number of techniques	(iii)	Incremental Budget

(d)	Budget prepared identifying current tasks independent of previous year	(iv)	Planning programming budgeting system

Codes :	**(a)**	**(b)**	**(c)**	**(d)**
(A)	iii	i	iv	ii
(B)	i	iii	iv	ii
(C)	iii	ii	i	iv
(D)	i	ii	iii	iv

ANSWERS

1 (c)	2 (a)	3 (c)	4 (d)
5 (c)	6 (c)	7 (c)	8 (a)
9 (b)	10 (b)	11 (a)	12 (a)
13 (c)	14 (d)	15 (a)	16 (a)
17 (c)	18 (a)	19 (c)	20 (c)
21 (d)	22 (a)	23 (b)	24 (b)
25 (c)	26 (d)	27 (b)	28 (a)
29 (c)	30 (d)	31 (d)	32 (a)
33 (b)	34 (a)	35 (b)	36 (b)
37 (a)	38 (c)	39 (c)	40 (d)
41 (d)	42 (a)	43 (b)	44 6
45 (b)	46 (a)	47 (d)	48 (c)
49 (b)	50 (c)	51 (c)	52 (a)
53 (c)	54 (a)	55 (b)	56 (a)
57 (c)	58 (b)	59 (a)	60 (d)
61 (c)	62 (b)	63 (b)	64 (a)
65 (b)	66 (c)	67 (c)	68 (b)
69 (b)	70 (c)	71 (b)	72 (d)
73 (a)	74 (b)	75 (a)	

December 2012

LIBRARY & INFORMATION SCIENCE

Paper – II

(1) According to Machlup the difference between information and knowledge is

(a) Information increases with use, whereas knowledge is constant.

(b) Information is stimulatory, whereas knowledge is practical.

(c) Information is shareable, whereas knowledge is one's property.

(d) Information is piecemeal, fragmented, particular, whereas knowledge is structured, coherent and universal.

(2) "Web of Science" is

(a) A Citation Index

(b) A Bibliography

(c) An Abstracting Service

(d) All of the above

(3) "Facts on File" can be grouped under

(a) Primary source (b) Secondary sourcc

(c) Tertiary source (d) None of the above

(4) In MARC 21, subject access fields are

(a) 3xx (b) 4xx

(c) 5xx (d) 6xx

(5) Transformation of traditional libraries to hybrid / digital libraries is

(a) Crisis Management

(b) Re-engineering

(c) Change Management

(d) Project Management

(6) Which one of the following is not a switching system?

(a) Packet (b) Circuit

(c) Router (d) Message

(7) Access to back volumes of E-journals is known as ______.

(a) Random Access (b) Perpetual Access

(c) Online Access (d) Retrospective Access

(8) The chi-square technique is used to compare the observed data with that of

(a) Collected raw data (b) Expected data

(c) Analysed data (d) Graphical data

(9) 'Parry Committee' (UK) was set up to advise

(a) School Libraries (b) Public Libraries

(c) Special Libraries (d) University Libraries

(10) FRBR is developed by

(a) LC (b) UNESCO

(c) IFLA (d) FID

(11) Who were involved in Public Library Movement in India ?

(i) Sayaji Rao Gaekwad II

(ii) C.D. Deshmukh

(iii) S. Radhakrishnan

(iv) S.R. Ranganathan

Codes :

(A) (i) & (iii) are correct (B) (ii) & (iv) are correct

(C) (i) & (iv) are correct (D) (ii) & (iii) are correct

(12) Which of the following are library networks ?

(i) Internet (ii) DELNET

(iii) NICNET (iv) OCLC

Codes :

(A) (i) and (ii) are correct.

(B) (ii) and (iv) are correct.

(C) (i) and (iii) are correct.

(D) (i) and (iv) are correct.

(13) Which of the following are review type services ?

(i) Current Awareness (ii) Trend Reports

(iii) News Clippings (iv) State of the Art Report

Codes :

(A) (i), (ii), (iii) are correct.

(B) (i), (iii), (iv) are correct.

(C) (ii) & (iv) are correct.

(D) (ii) & (iii) are correct.

(14) The basic characteristics of a system are

(i) Interrelated components

(ii) Independent and can stand alone

(iii) Arranged in hierarchical order

(iv) Inputs, processes, outputs & feed back

Codes :

(A) (i), (ii), (iii) are correct.

(B) (i), (ii), (iv) are correct

(C) (ii), (iii), (iv) are correct.

(D) (i), (iii), (iv) are correct.

(15) The general image file formats are :

(i) TIFF (ii) JPEG

(iii) MPEG (iv) PNG

Codes :

(A) (i), (ii) and (iii) are correct.

(B) (i), (iii) and (iv) are correct

(C) (i), (ii) and (iv) are correct.

(D) (ii), (iii) and (iv) are correct.

(16) Which of the following are common types of protocols?

(i) HTTP (ii) FTP

(iii) Telnet (iv) Gopher

Codes :

(A) (i) and (ii) are correct.

(B) (i), (ii) and (iv) are correct.

(C) (iii) and (iv) are correct.

(D) (i), (ii) and (iii) are correct.

(17) Which of the following are not the elements of DOI system ?

(i) Policies (ii) Subject

(iii) Description (iv) Resolution

Codes :

(A) (i), (ii) and (iii) are correct.

(B) (i), (iii) and (iv) are correct.

(C) (i), (ii) and (iv) are correct.

(D) (ii), (iii) and (iv) are correct

(18) Which of the following are Trade Bibliographies ?

(i) Books-in-Print

(ii) Indian Books-in-Print

(iii) Indian National Bibliography

(iv) British National Bibliography

Codes :

(A) (i) and (iii) are correct.

(B) (ii) and (iv) are correct

(C) (i) and (ii) are correct.

(D) (ii) and (iii) are correct.

(19) **Assertion (A) :** Distance education for LIS courses is gaining ground in India.

Reason (R) : Majority of people prefer it as an alternative channel of education.

Codes :

(A) (A) is true but (R) is false.

(B) (A) is false but (R) is true.

(C) Both (A) and (R) are correct.

(D) Both (A) and (R) are wrong.

(20) **Assertion (A) :** Indian libraries are making optimum use of social networking.

Reason (R) : Social networking has wider role in dissemination of information.

Codes :

(A) (A) is true but (R) is false.

(B) (A) is false but (R) is true.

(C) (A) and (R) both are true.

(D) (A) and (R) both are false.

(21) **Assertion (A) :** Knowledge is growing exponentially.

Reason (R) : Number of researchers have increased.

Codes :

(A) Both (A) & (R) are true.

(B) Both (A) and (R) are false.

(C) (A) is false but (R) is true.

(D) (A) is true but (R) is false.

(22) **Assertion (A) :** Present decade has accepted E-journals as channels of fast communication.

Reason (R) : E-publications have added enormous quantity of literature but affected the quality of research.

Codes :

(A) (A) is true but (R) is false.

(B) (A) is false but (R) is true

(C) Both (A) and (R) are true and (R) is the correct explanation

(D) Both (A) and (R) are true, but (R) is not a correct explanation

(23) **Assertion (A) :** Library & Information centres are knowledge/ management centres.

Reason (R) : Libraries handle tacit knowledge.

Codes :

(A) Both (A) and (R) are true

(B) (A) is partially true, but (R) is false

(C) (A) is false, but (R) is true

(D) Both (A) and (R) are false

(24) **Assertion (A) :** Metadata hold much promise for information retrieval and access in the digital age.

Reason (R) : Metadata can save a number of functions including description, resource discovery and management of resources.

Codes :

(A) (A) is true, but (R) is false.

(B) (A) is false, but (R) is true.

(C) Both (A) and (R) are true.

(D) Both (A) and (R) are false.

(25) **Assertion (A) :** Training methods through brain storming stimulate idea generation.

Reason (R) : Training methods do not provide opportunity to unskilled to become skilled.

Codes :

(A) (A) is false but (R) is true.

(B) Both (A) and (R) are false.

(C) Both (A) and (R) are true.

(D) (A) is true but (R) is false.

(26) **Assertion (A) :** Random samples are not representative of the whole population.

Reason (R) : Random numbers are used in forming a random sample.

Codes :

(A) (A) is true, but (R) is false.

(B) Both (A) and (R) are true.

(C) (A) is false, but (R) is true.

(D) Both (A) and (R) are false.

(27) **Assertion (A) :** Information Literacy is a basic skill essential for work environment in 21st century.

Reason (R) : Information Literacy helps to train the users to make use of ICT.

Codes :

(A) Both (A) and (R) are true

(B) Both (A) and (R) are false

(C) (A) is true, but (R) is false

(D) (A) is false, but (R) is true

(28) Arrange the following according to their year of first publication :

(i) Bliss Classification

(ii) Library of Congress Classification

(iii) Dewey Decimal Classification

(iv) Universal Decimal Classification

Codes :

(A) (i), (ii), (iii), (iv) (B) (i), (iii), (ii), (iv)

(C) (iii), (i), (iv), (ii) (D) (ii), (iv), (i), (iii)

(29) Arrange the following IFLA programmes according to their year of commencement :

(i) UBC (iii) ISBD

(ii) UAP (iv) International MARC Office

Codes :

(A) (i), (iv), (iii), (ii) (B) (ii), (iv), (i), (iii)

(C) (iv), (i), (ii), (iii) (D) (iii), (i), (ii), (iv)

(30) Arrange the following according to their year of origin:

(i) Indian National Bibliography

(ii) Cumulative Book Index

(iii) British National Bibliography

(iv) Books in Print

Codes :

(A) (i), (iii), (iv), (ii) (B) (ii), (i), (iii), (iv)

(C) (iv), (iii), (ii), (i) (D) (iii), (iv), (ii), (i)

(31) Arrange the following in a chronological order according to their year of establishment :

(i) Library of Congress (ii) Delivery of Books Act

(iii) NISCAIR (iv) National Library of India

Codes :

(A) (iii), (iv), (ii), (i) (B) (ii), (iii), (i), (iv)

(C) (i), (iv), (iii), (ii) (D) (iv), (i), (iii), (ii)

(32) Arrange the following bibliographical standards according to their year of development :

(i) ISBD (ii) Dublin Core

(iii) MARC (iv) RDF

Codes :

(A) (i), (iii), (ii), (iv) (B) (ii), (i), (iv), (iii)

(C) (iii), (ii), (iv), (i) (D) (iv), (iii), (i), (ii)

(33) Arrange the following according to their year of origin:

(i) UNICODE (ii) HTML

(iii) XML (iv) SGML

Codes :

(A) (iv), (iii), (i), (ii) (B) (iii), (iv), (ii), (i)

(C) (ii), (iv), (i), (iii) (D) (i), (ii), (iii), (iv)

(34) Arrange the following in order of their year of establishment :

(i) INIS (ii) MEDLARS

(iii) AGRIS (iv) UNESCO

Codes :

(A) (iii), (i), (iv), (ii) (B) (ii), (iv), (i), (iii)

(C) (iv), (iii), (ii), (i) (D) (i), (ii), (iv), (iii)

(35) Arrange the following according to their year of enactment :

(i) Tamil Nadu Public Library Act

(ii) Kerala Public Library Act

(iii) Maharashtra Public Library Act

(iv) Orissa Public Library Act

Codes :

(A) (i), (iii), (ii), (iv) (B) (ii), (iii), (iv), (i)

(C) (ii), (iii), (i), (iv) (D) (iv), (iii), (ii), (i)

(36) Match the following :

	List – I	**List – II**
(a)	'Guide to Use of Books And Libraries'	(i) F.W. Lancaster
(b)	'If You Want to Evaluate Your Library'	(ii) A.C. Foskelt
(c)	'Cuneiform to Computer: A History of Reference Sources'	(iii) Jean K. Gates
(d)	'Subject Approach to Information'	(iv) William A. Katz

Codes :	**(a)**	**(b)**	**(c)**	**(d)**
(A)	ii	iii	iv	i
(B)	i	iv	iii	ii
(C)	iii	i	iv	ii
(D)	iv	ii	i	iii

(37) Match the following :

	List – I		**List – II**
(a)	Directory	(i)	Information Please Almanac
(b)	Annuals	(ii)	Keesing's Record of World Events
(c)	Bibliography	(iii)	Encyclopaedia of Associations
(d)	News paper Digest	(iv)	Publishers' Weekly

Codes :	**(a)**	**(b)**	**(c)**	**(d)**
(A)	iii	i	iv	ii
(B)	i	iii	iv	ii
(C)	iii	ii	iv	i
(D)	iv	i	ii	iii

(38) Match the following :

	List – I		**List – II**
(a)	Guiding users to the place of information	(i)	Digest
(b)	Guiding users in the use of information	(ii)	User orientation
(c)	Alerting users with the latest arrivals	(iii)	Referral
(d)	Providing users with summarized information	(iv)	Current Awareness

Codes :	**(a)**	**(b)**	**(c)**	**(d)**
(A)	iii	iv	i	ii
(B)	iii	ii	iv	i
(C)	iv	i	iii	ii
(D)	ii	i	iii	iv

(39) Match the following :

	List – I		List – II
(a)	B.S. Kesvan	(i)	School of librarianship
(b)	Paul Otlet	(ii)	National Library of India
(c)	W.C.B. Sayers	(iii)	UDC
(d)	M. Taube	(iv)	Uniterm Indexing

Codes :	**(a)**	**(b)**	**(c)**	**(d)**
(A)	ii	iii	i	iv
(B)	iii	ii	i	iv
(C)	ii	iii	iv	i
(D)	iv	ii	iii	i

(40) Match the following :

	List – I		List – II
(a)	Theory of Motivation	(i)	Factor of planning
(b)	Unity of Command	(ii)	Efficiency and waste prevention
(c)	MBO	(iii)	Maslow
(d)	Forecasting	(iv)	Peter Drucker

Codes :	**(a)**	**(b)**	**(c)**	**(d)**
(A)	i	ii	iii	iv
(B)	iv	i	ii	iii
(C)	ii	iii	iv	i
(D)	iii	iv	i	ii

(41) Match the following :

	List – I		List – II
(a)	Classification	(i)	LISA
(b)	Cataloguing	(ii)	UDC
(c)	Subject Heading	(iii)	AACR
(d)	Library Science Abstracts	(iv)	LCSH

Codes :	(a)	(b)	(c)	(d)
(A)	ii	i	iv	iii
(B)	ii	iii	iv	i
(C)	iv	iii	i	ii
(D)	ii	iv	i	iii

(42) Match the following :

List – I (Budgetary technique)	List – II (Limitation of budgetary technique)
(a) Line	(i) Detailed information required
(b) Formula	(ii) Time consuming
(c) PPBS	(iii) Do not permit variation
(d) Zerobased	(iv) Do not suggest future

Codes :	(a)	(b)	(c)	(d)
(A)	ii	i	iv	iii
(B)	iii	ii	i	iv
(C)	iv	iii	i	ii
(D)	i	iv	ii	iii

(43) Match the following :

List – I	List – II
(a) File transfer protocol	(i) Data transmission capacity
(b) Multimedia	(ii) Integration of text, colour sound and animation
(c) Bandwidth	(iii) Bulletin Board
(d) Electronic Notice Board	(iv) Internet

Codes :	(a)	(b)	(c)	(d)
(A)	iv	ii	i	iii
(B)	i	iii	ii	iv
(C)	ii	i	iv	iii
(D)	i	iv	ii	iii

(44) Match the following :

	List – I		List – II
(a)	ISDN	(i)	Web page
(b)	URL	(ii)	Video Conferencing
(c)	Firewall	(iii)	Internet Standard for Information Transmission
(d)	HTTP	(iv)	Protecting unauthorized access internet

Codes :	(a)	(b)	(c)	(d)
(A)	iii	iv	i	ii
(B)	iv	i	iii	ii
(C)	ii	i	iv	iii
(D)	i	iii	ii	iv

(45) Match the following :

	List – I		List – II
(a)	OCLC	(i)	Bio-Med
(b)	INFLIBNET	(ii)	Web-Dewey
(c)	IISC	(iii)	N-List
(d)	NLM	(iv)	Digital Library of India

Codes :	(a)	(b)	(c)	(d)
(A)	ii	iii	iv	i
(B)	iii	i	ii	iv
(C)	iv	ii	iii	i
(D)	i	iii	iv	ii

Read the passage given below, and answer the questions based on your understanding of the passage. (Question Nos. **46-50**) With the realization across the world that the global economy is going to be increasingly knowledge-based, science and technology have become the subject of discussion not just in classical ministries but also in ministries as diverse as commerce, industry and finance, and in case of United States, even in the State Department. In India,the Prime Minister has made frequent statements about the need to step up scientific research in the country. Several large companies, including multinationals are outsourcing R & D programmes to India. This is partly because scientists are cheaper in India dollar for dollar, put also because India has a large pool of trained scientists. Industry data shows that R & D is now the third-largest segment in India's export of Information Technology (IT) services. Foreign companies have invested over $ 1 billion in research operations in India from 1998 to 2003 and another estimated $ 5 billion are in the pipeline. The United States is the biggest investor followed by Germany, France, Denmark and UK. Japan and China have also begun to invest in research programmes in India. Most foreign investment is being directed to research in computer sciences, pharmaceuticals, molecular chemistry, drug discovery, engineering and automotive design and biotechnology, including plant breeding.Whereas, flow of foreign investments has enthused research institutions that are targeted for collaboration, there is also cause for concern. Although, India now attracts considerable foreign investment in R & D, it has no system in place for assessing how this investment is affecting the country's technological development. Nor is there any mechanism to monitorthe impact of such investment on aspects such as skill development, sectoral capacity building etc. Do such foreign – funded research programmes benefit only the scientists and technicians in the form of better salaries and perks or do they also produce benefits for the country as a whole ?

(46) Focus on science and technology has increased because

(A) Indian commerce and Finance Ministries are giving great importance to it

(B) World economy has become knowledge based

(C) US State Department gives priority on S & T

(D) Knowledge Commission has identified it as one of the potential area of development

(47) The following group of countries are the biggest investors in research :

(A) U.S., Germany, India, Russia

(B) Britain, France, U.S., India

(C) France, Denmark, U.S.A., U.K

(D) Japan, China, India, Denmark

(48) What is the cause of concern regarding foreign investment in research ?

(A) Scientists and technicians involved in research are not paid well

(B) There are insufficient institutions that can be targeted for research collaboration.

(C) The benefit of such investments doesn't get transferred to India.

(D) Sufficient methods to assess and evaluate the impact of such investment are not available.

(49) Most foreign investment is being made in the area of

(A) Microbiology and life sciences.

(B) Computer science and automotive design

(C) Physical sciences and planting

(D) Grafting and biology

(50) Foreign companies are outsourcing R & D programmes to India because

(A) Quality of research is quite high in India.

(B) Outsourcing is cost effective for foreign companies

(C) There is scarcity of skilled manpower in those countries

(D) None of the above

ANSWERS

01 (d)	02 (a)	03 (b)	04 (d)
05 (c)	06 (c)	07 (b)	08 (b)
09 (d)	10 (c)	11 (c)	12 (b)
13 (c)	14 (d)	15 (c)	16 (d)
17 (b)	18 (c)	19 (c)	20 (b)
21 (a)	22 (c)	23 (b)	24 (c)
25 (d)	26 (b)	27 (c)	28 (b)
29 (c)	30 (d)	31 (c)	32 (b)
33 (a)	34 (c)	35 (a)	36 (c)
37 (a)	38 (b)	39 (a)	40 (d)
41 (b)	42 (c)	43 (a)	44 (c)
45 (a)	46 (b)	47 (c)	48 (d)
49 (b)	50 (b)		

December 2012

LIBRARY AND INFORMATION SCIENCE

Paper – III

(1) Who categorized the user studies into the following three categories ?

(i) Behaviour Studies

(ii) Use studies

(iii) Information flow studies

(a) Maurice B Line (b) Menzel

(c) Cronin (d) Voigt

(2) Which one of the following is not a virtual library ?

(a) Without walls.

(b) With distributed physicallocations.

(c) Providing integrated andunified remote access to geographically distributedcollections.

(d) Which does not exist in reality.

(3) In 1974, Zurkowski used for the first time, which of the following term ?

(a) Digital Literacy (b) Media Literacy

(c) Computer Literacy (d) Information Literacy

(4) Who defined "to be information literate, a person must be able to recognize when information is needed and have the ability to locate, evaluate and use effectively the needed information." ?

(a) SLA (b) ALA

(c) IFLA (d) CILIP

(5) Which of the factor is not helping in limiting the external validity ?

(a) Reactive effect (b) Ecological validity

(c) Interaction between selection bias of experimental variables

(d) Ecological effect

(6) Semantic differential scale is concerned with

(a) Pool of items

(b) Selection from two opposite position

(c) Five point scale

(d) Selection from a check list

(7) In spiral of scientific method, the span of Zenith to descendent is

(a) Empirical phase (b) Hypothesizing phase

(c) Deductive phase (d) Verification phase

(8) Which of the following variable cannot be expressed in quantitative terms ?

(a) Socio-Economic status

(b) Marital status

(c) Numerical Aptitude

(d) Professional Attitude

(9) National Knowledge Network is to be implemented by

(a) National KnowledgeCommission

(b) Information and LibraryNetwork

(c) National Information Centre

(d) Department of InformationTechnology

(10) Metadata Dublin core refers to

(a) Data elements in database

(b) Bibliographic elements indatabase

(c) Field elements in database

(d) Subject elements in database

(11) E-Journal articles can be identified with the help of

(a) Digital Journal Identifier

(b) Journal Source Identifier

(c) Journal Article Identifier

(d) Digital Object Identifier

(12) Z39.50 is a standard for

(a) Communication formats

(b) Search and Retrieval services

(c) Cataloguing Web Resources

(d) Library Management Services

(13) In context to modulation, PCM stands for

(a) Pulse Code Modulation

(b) Phase Control Modulation

(c) Popular Code Modulation

(d) Penultimate Code Modulation

(14) ISO 9000 standard denotes the

(a) consistence confirmance of a product or service to a given set of standard or expectations

(b) Total customer satisfaction

(c) Representation of stakeholders issues.

(d) Detailed list of measuring techniques

(15) The stages in the product life cycle curve are

(a) Introduction, Growth, Maturity, Decline

(b) Introduction, Growth, Maturity,Profit

(c) Growth, Maturity, Profit, Decline

(d) Introduction, Growth, Maturity,Saturation

(16) The physical and chemical treatment of materials to retard their further deterioration refers to

(a) Conservation (b) Rescuing

(c) Prevention (d) Restoration

(17) Read the following example and indicate the name of the indexing system used: 'Remuneration of teachers in French universities.' The index headings are set as the following two lines :

France Universities Teachers Remuneration

Universities FranceTeachers Remuneration

(a) Chain procedure (b) POPSI

(c) PRECIS (d) KWIC

(18) Research in automatic classification for information retrieval of term or cluster of terms is called

(a) Evaluation theory (b) Theory of clumps

(c) Time binding theory (d) Dynamic theory

(19) As specified by AACR-II (R), the source of information for machine readable data file is

(a) Internal user label (b) Title page

(c) Colophone (d) Title frame

(20) NICRYS is information system for

(a) Machine tools (b) Food science

(c) Crystallography (d) Drugs

(21) The national convention regularly organized by DELNET is known as

(a) CALIBER (b) ICDL

(c) NACLIN (d) DELNETCON

(22) Report on 'the development of digital libraries of the past decade' is categorized as

(a) Review Report (b) Trend Report

(c) Research Report (d) State of the art report

(23) Name of the President of Sri Lanka can be found in

(a) International who's who

(b) Stateman's Yearbook

(c) Who's who in the world

(d) Wilson Biographies

(24) Which of the following has stopped publishing in the print from since 2012 ?

(a) Europa World Yearbook

(b) Times of India Directory

(c) New Encyclopedia Britannica

(d) Keesing's ContemporaryArchives

(25) Which of the following is not providing encyclopedia type of information ?

(a) Encyclopedia of Associations

(b) Compton's Encyclopedia

(c) Worldbook Encyclopedia

(d) Encyclopedia Americana

(26) Who used the phrase 'control-access directional type sources' ?

(a) R.E. Bopp (b) B.C. Wynar

(c) W.A. Katz (d) R. Balay

(27) Raja Rammohan Roy Library Foundation (RRRLF) was established by

(a) Indian Library Association

(b) Department of Culture, Govt.of India

(c) Govt. of West Bengal

(d) Ministry of Home Affairs,Govt. of India

(28) Which State Public Library Act has the provision to collect library fund through land tax ?

(a) Tamil Nadu (b) Karnataka

(c) Andhra Pradesh (d) Maharashtra

(29) Association of College and Research Libraries (ACRL) (USA) is a

(a) Division of American Library Association

(b) Independent Association forAcademic & ResearchLibraries

(c) Division of Special LibrariesAssociation (USA)

(d) Division of IFLA

(30) Which of the following is not an implication of Fourth Law of Library Science?

(a) Classified arrangement

(b) Stack-room-guides

(c) Issue Methods

(d) Rural Library Services

(31) Which one of the following is not a recommendation of National Knowledge Commission (India) ?

(a) Preparation of a NationalCensus of Library

(b) Encourage greater communityparticipation in librarymanagement

(c) Raja Rammohan Roy libraryfoundation to act as theNational co-ordination agency

(d) Facilitate donation andmaintenance of privatecollection

(32) Digital library function incorporate :

(i) Creating and capturing

(ii) Storage and management

(iii) Search and access

(iv) Abstracting and reviewing

Codes :

(a) (ii), (iii) and (iv) are correct.

(b) (i), (iii) and (iv) are correct.

(c) (i), (ii) and (iii) are correct.

(d) (i), (ii) and (iv) are correct.

(33) Which topology of computer network provides faster server access ?

(i) BUS Network Topology

(ii) RING Network Topology

(iii) MULTIPLE RING Network Topology

(iv) STAR Network Topology

Codes :

(a) (i) and (ii) are correct.

(b) (i) and (iii) are correct.

(c) (ii) and (iii) are correct.

(d) (ii) and (iv) are correct.

(34) Which of the following are ISDN services ?

(i) RSS (ii) Teletext

(iii) Voice mail (iv) Video conference

Codes :

(a) (i), (iii) and (iv) are correct.

(b) (i), (ii) and (iv) are correct.

(c) (ii), (iii) and (iv) are correct.

(d) (i), (ii) and (iii) are correct

(35) Vocabulary in a database is controlled by :

(i) Import files (ii) Thesaurus files

(iii) Standard files (iv) Authority files

Codes :

(a) (i) and (ii) are correct.

(b) (iii) and (iv) are correct.

(c) (i) and (iii) are correct.

(d) (ii) and (iii) are correct.

(36) CCF for bibliographic record refers to

(i) Data transfer

(ii) Data storage

(iii) Standard tags of data Identification

(iv) Formatting of records

Codes :

(a) (i) and (iii) are correct

(b) (i), (ii) and (iv) are correct

(c) (ii) and (iii) are correct.

(d) (iii), (i) and (ii) are correct.

(37) Which of the following are not reference service ?

(i) Preparation of user profile

(ii) Initiation of freshman

(iii) Compilation of documentation list

(iv) Readers Advisory

Codes :

(a) (i) and (ii) (b) (ii) and (iii)

(c) (i) and (iii) (d) (iii) and (iv)

(38) Which of the following functions are analysed by ALA as reference service functions ?

(i) Consultation function

(ii) Guidance function

(iii) Instruction function

(iv) Bibliographic function

Codes:

(a) (i), (ii) and (iii) are correct.

(b) (ii), (iii) and (iv) are correct.

(c) (i), (ii) and (iv) are correct.

(d) (i), (iii) and (iv) are correct.

(39) Which of the following are the scientists' approach according to Melvin J. Voigt (1961) ?

(i) Current Approach

(ii) Everyday Approach

(iii) Exhaustive Approach

(iv) 'Catching up' or 'brushing up'approach.

Codes:

(a) (ii), (iii) and (iv) (b) (i), (iii) and (iv)

(c) (i), (ii) and (iv) (d) (i), (ii) and (iii)

(40) Magazines are suitable for

(i) Leisure and entertainment

(ii) Scholarly information

(iii) Popular information

(iv) Subject information

Codes:

(a) (i), (ii) and (iii) are correct.

(b) (ii), (iii) and (iv) are correct.

(c) (i) and (iii) are correct.

(d) (ii) and (iv) are correct.

(41) Planting the virus 'Trojan Horse' in computer network is

(i) Hacking (ii) Tampering

(iii) Decryption (iv) Intrusion

Codes :

(a) (i), (iii) and (iv) are correct

(b) (ii), (iii) and (iv) are correct

(c) (i), (ii) and (iii) are correct

(d) (i), (ii) and (iv) are correct

(42) Which of the following are the fundamental conditions for a subject to be protected by IPR ?

(i) The work must be original

(ii) The work must be man made

(iii) The work must be intelligible

(iv) The work must be recorded/ fixed

Codes :

(a) (i), (ii) and (iii) are correct.

(b) (i), (iii) and (iv) are correct.

(c) (ii), (iii) and (iv) are correct.

(d) (i), (ii) and (iv) are correct

(43) Which of the following are the problems of present information environment ?

(i) Information indiscipline

(ii) Information literacy

(iii) Information overload

(iv) Information technology

Codes:

(a) (i), (iii) are correct

(b) (i) and (iv) are correct

(c) (ii) and (iv) are correct

(d) (i) and (ii) are correct

(44) **Assertion (A) :** Qualitative measures must be made quantifiable in order to be convincing.

Reason (R) : Qualitative measures are a necessary complement to quantitative measures.

Codes :

(a) is true, (R) is false.

(b) (A) is false, (R) is true.

(c) Both (A) & (R) are true.

(d) Both (A) & (R) are false.

(45) Which of the following are not partners of National Programme on Technology Enhanced Learning (NPTEL) ?

(i) IIT Madras (ii) IIT Delhi

(iii) IIIT Bangalore (iv) NIT Rourkela

Codes:

(a) (iii) and (iv) (b) (i) and (iv)

(c) (ii) and (iii) (d) (i) and (ii)

(46) **Assertion (A) :** Internet can replace libraries.

Reason (R) : Google searches will satisfy the maximum users needs.

Codes:

(a) Both (A) and (R) are true.

(b) Both (A) and (R) are false.

(c) (A) is true but (R) is false.

(d) (A) is false but (R) is true.

(47) **Assertion (A) :** Federated search technique is an integral component of an information portal.

Reason (R) : 'Content Index' contains content that is find by the search server.

Codes:

(a) Both (A) and (R) are true.

(b) Both (A) and (R) are false.

(c) (A) is true but (R) is false.

(d) (A) is false but (R) is true

(48) **Assertion (A) :** A combination of hypertext and Hypermedia contains text, images, sounds and other information.

Reason (R) : Hypermedia information is represented in a linear fashion.

Codes:

(a) (A) is true and (R) is false.

(b) Both (A) and (R) are true.

(c) (A) is false and (R) is true.

(d) Both (A) & (R) are false.

(49) **Assertion (A) :** Book selection should be done judiciously.

Reason (R) : A library should acquire important and latest book selection tools.

Codes:

(a) (A) is true but (R) is false.

(b) (A) is false but (R) is true.

(c) Both (A) & (R) are true, but(R) is not the correct explanation of (A).

(d) Both (A) & (R) are true and (R)is the correct explanation of (A)

(50) **Assertion (A) :** TQM promotes the way in which a library is organised and perform its ICT functions.

Reason (R) : TQM is seen as a hindrance to library and information services.

Codes:

(a) Both (A) and (R) are true.

(b) Both (A) and (R) are false.

(c) (A) is false and (R) is true.

(d) (A) is true and (R) is false

(51) **Assertion (A) :** The array of classes 11, 12, 13 and the array of classes 31, 32, 33 are said to be collateral arrays.

Reason (R) : They are derived from the original universe 'O'.

Codes:

(a) (A) is false, (R) is true.

(b) (A) is true, (R) is false.

(c) Both (A) & (R) are true.

(d) Both (A) & (R) are false.

(52) **Assertion (A) :** RDF supports the use and exchange of metadata on the web.

Reason (R) : Bibliographic standards are the means to create and disseminate secondary information.

Codes:

(a) (A) is true, (R) is false.

(b) (A) is false, (R) is true.

(c) Both (A) & (R) are correct.

(d) Both (A) & (R) are false.

(53) **Assertion (A) :** Informative abstracts provide a concise summary of the subject content of an article.

Reason (R) : These are title oriented than finding-oriented

Codes:

(a) Both (A) and (R) are true.

(b) (A) is true but (R) is false.

(c) (A) is false but (R) is true.

(d) Both (A) and (R) are false.

(54) **Assertion (A) :** E-publications have added enormous quantity of literature but adversely affected the quality of literature.

Reason (R) : Present decade has accepted E-publication as channels of fast communication.

Codes:

(a) (A) is true (R) is false.

(b) (A) is false, but (R) is correct

(c) Both (A) & (R) are false.

(d) Both (A) & (R) are true.

(55) **Assertion (A) :** Encyclopedias are not relevant for finding geographically information.

Reason (R) : Encyclopedias are the substitute for all categories of reference sources.

Codes:

(a) (A) is false but (R) is true

(b) Both (A) and (R) are true.

(c) Both (A) and (R) are false.

(d) (A) is true but (R) is false.

(56) **Assertion (A) :** LIS profession is not considered at par with medical and legal professions.

Reason (R) : There is no constitutional body for LIS profession like Medical Council of India (MCI) and Bar Council of India (BCI).

Codes:

(a) Both (A) and (R) are true.

(b) Both (A) and (R) are false.

(c) (A) is true but (R) is false.

(d) (A) is false but (R) is true.

(57) **Assertion (A) :** Dr. S.R. Ranganathan has been called 'Father of Library and Information Science' in India.

Reason (R) : Library Science education in India was started by Dr. S.R. Ranganathan.

Codes:

(a) (A) is false but (R) is true.

(b) (A) is true but (R) is false.

(c) Both (A) and (R) are true.

(d) Both (A) and (R) are false.

(58) **Assertion (A) :** The exclusive rights conferred by Intellectual property rights can generally be transferred / licenced to third parties.

Reason (R) : The creators want to make monetary benefits out of their intellectual product.

Codes:

(a) (A) is true but (R) is false

(b) (A) is false but (R) is true.

(c) Both (A) & (R) are true.

(d) Both (A) & (R) are false

(59) Which is the correct sequence of the national libraries in the order of their year of establishment?

(i) British Library (formerly British Museum Library)

(ii) Library of Congress(Washington D.C.)

(iii) Lenin Library (Moscow)

(iv) Bibliotheque Nationale (Paris)

Codes :

(A) (i), (ii), (iii), (iv) (B) (ii), (iii), (i), (iv)

(C) (iii), (ii), (iv), (i) (D) (iv), (iii), (ii), (i)

(60) What is the correct order of SCONUL's "Seven Pillar Model of Information Skills" ?

(i) Recognise information need

(ii) Construct strategies forLocating

(iii) Compare and evaluate

(iv) Locate and access

Codes :

(A) (i), (ii), (iii), (iv) (B) (ii), (iii), (iv), (i)

(C) (i), (ii), (iv), (iii) (D) (ii), (iii), (i), (iv)

(61) Identify the correct order as per increasing data storage capacity :

(a) CDROM, DVD, Cartridge, Blue Ray Disc

(b) DVD, Cartridge, BlueRay Disc,CDROM

(c) Cartridge, CDROM, DVD, Blue Ray Disc

(d) BlueRay Disc, DVD, Cartridge, CDROM

(62) Identify the correct order of the LIS Associations as per their year ofEstablishment

(a) CLA, ALA, SLA, IASLIC

(b) ALA, SLA, CLA, IASLIC

(c) SLA, IASLIC, ALA, CLA

(d) CLA, SLA, IASLIC, ALA

(63) Arrange the following State Library Acts in chronological order :

(i) Karnataka Public Library Act

(ii) Uttar Pradesh Public LibraryAct

(iii) Goa Public Library Act

(iv) Bihar Public Library Act

Codes :

(A) (i), (iii), (ii), (iv) (B) (i), (ii), (iii), (iv)

(C) (ii), (iii), (iv), (i) (D) (iii), (i), (iv), (ii)

(64) Match the following :

	List – I		**List – II**
(a)	Mean	(i)	Most Frequently occurring value
(b)	Mode	(ii)	Average
(c)	Median	(iii)	Measure of dispersion
(d)	Standard Deviation	(iv)	Middle Value

Codes :	**(a)**	**(b)**	**(c)**	**(d)**
(A)	iii	iv	i	ii
(B)	ii	i	iv	iii
(C)	iv	iii	i	ii
(D)	ii	iii	iv	i

(65) Match the following :

	List – I		**List – II**
(a)	Bradford	(i)	Citation indexing
(b)	Lotka	(ii)	Distribution of Articles published in periodicals
(c)	Zipf	(iii)	Scientific productivity of author
(d)	Garfield	(iv)	Frequency of word occurrencein a text

Codes :	**(a)**	**(b)**	**(c)**	**(d)**
(A)	iv	i	iii	ii
(B)	ii	iii	iv	i
(C)	iii	iv	i	ii
(D)	iv	iii	ii	i

(66) Match the following

List – I	**List – II**
(a) Altavista	(i) Subject search engine
(b) Lycos	(ii) Meta search engine
(c) Geoindex	(iii) Regional search engine
(d) Savvysearch	(iv) General search engine

Codes :	**(a)**	**(b)**	**(c)**	**(d)**
(A)	iii	ii	i	iv
(B)	iii	iv	ii	i
(C)	iv	iii	i	ii
(D)	iv	i	ii	iii

(67) Match the following :

List – I	**List – II**
(a) Pen drive	(i) Communication
(b) i-Pad	(ii) Web server device
(c) Wifi Modem	(iii) Storage device
(d) Cloud computing	(iv) Computing device

Codes :	**(a)**	**(b)**	**(c)**	**(d)**
(A)	i	iii	ii	iv
(B)	iii	iv	i	ii
(C)	iv	iii	ii	i
(D)	iii	ii	i	iv

(68) Match the following :

	List – I		List – II
(a)	Informix	(i)	Image software
(b)	Omni Page	(ii)	Remote login software
(c)	TIFF viewer	(iii)	DBMS software
(d)	Team Viewer	(iv)	OCR software

Codes :	(a)	(b)	(c)	(d)
(A)	ii	i	iii	iv
(B)	iii	iv	i	ii
(C)	i	ii	iii	iv
(D)	iv	iii	ii	i

(69) Match the following :

	List – I		List – II
(a)	Means of improving operations and services	(i)	Preservation
(b)	Preparation of to-do-list	(ii)	Standards
(c)	Performance guidelines	(iii)	Time management
(d)	Reinforce the spines of books	(iv)	Evaluation

Codes :	(a)	(b)	(c)	(d)
(A)	iv	iii	ii	i
(B)	iv	ii	iii	i
(C)	ii	iv	iii	i
(D)	iii	ii	i	iv

(70) Match the following :

	List – I		List – II
(a)	Chain indexing	(i)	Derek Austin
(b)	Relational indexing	(ii)	S.R. Ranganathan
(c)	Subject Indexing	(iii)	J.E.L. Farradane
(d)	PRECIS	(iv)	E.J. Coats

Codes :	(a)	(b)	(c)	(d)
(A)	i	ii	iv	iii
(B)	ii	iii	iv	i
(C)	i	ii	iii	iv
(D)	ii	iv	i	iii

(71) Match the following :

	List – I		List – II
(A)	Collateral classes	(i)	Class comprising two or more entities
(B)	Multiple classes	(ii)	Classes of the same order but not belonging to one in the same order
(C)	Chain of classes	(iii)	A subject fixed with others in the universal of subject
(D)	Co-ordinate classes	(iv)	A sequence of classes made upof any given class and its universe

Codes :	(A)	(B)	(C)	(D)
(a)	ii	iv	i	iii
(b)	i	iii	ii	iv
(c)	ii	i	iv	iii
(d)	i	iv	ii	iii

(72) **72.** Match the following :

	List – I		List – II
(a)	William Martin	(i)	Little Science Big Science
(b)	Alvin Toffler	(ii)	Information society
(c)	Eric J de Solla Price	(iii)	Documentation
(d)	S.C. Bradford	(iv)	The Third Wave

Codes :	(a)	(b)	(c)	(d)
(A)	ii	iv	i	iii
(B)	iv	ii	iii	i
(C)	ii	iv	i	iii
(D)	i	iv	ii	iii

(73) Match the following :

	List – I	List – II
(a)	Communication Barrier	(i) Radio
(b)	Communication Medium	(ii) Shanon & Weaver
(c)	Communication Model	(iii) Video-conferencing
(d)	Interactive Communication	(iv) Noise

Codes :	(a)	(b)	(c)	(d)
(A)	ii	iv	iii	i
(B)	iv	ii	iii	i
(C)	ii	iv	i	iii
(D)	i	iv	ii	iii

(74) Match the following :

	List – I	List – II
(a)	Osgood and Schramm	(i) General Model
(b)	Berlo	(ii) Mathematical Model
(c)	Shannon and Weaver	(iii) Circular Model
(d)	George Gerbner	(iv) S-M-C-R Model

Codes :	(a)	(b)	(c)	(d)
(A)	i	ii	iii	iv
(B)	ii	iii	iv	i
(C)	iii	iv	ii	i
(D)	iv	i	ii	iii

(75) Match the following :

List – I	List – II
(a) Information contribution to the GNP of a nation	(i) Social information
(b) Information that changes human activity	(ii) Technological information
(c) Information that establishes interaction between government and people	(iii) Economic information
(d) Information that forms a modern society	(iv) Political information

Codes :	(a)	(b)	(c)	(d)
(A)	iii	i	iv	ii
(B)	i	iii	iv	ii
(C)	iv	ii	i	iii
(D)	ii	iii	iv	i

ANSWERS

1 (b)	2 (b)	3 (d)	4 (b)
5 (d)	6 (b)	7 (c)	8 (d)
9 (c)	10 (a)	11 (d)	12 (b)
13 (a)	14 (a)	15 (c)	16 (a)
17 (c)	18 (b)	19 (a)	20 (c)
21 (c)	22 (b)	23 (b)	24 (c)
25 (a)	26 (c)	27 (b)	28 (b)
29 (a)	30 (d)	31 (c)	32 (a)
33 (d)	34 (c)	35 (b)	36 (a)
37 (c)	38 (b)	39 (d)	40 (c)
41 (b)	42 (d)	43 (a)	44 (c)
45 (a)	46 (b)	47 (c)	48 (a)
49 (c)	50 (d)	51 (b)	52 (c)

53 (b)	54 (d)	55 (b)	56 (a)
57 (b)	58 (c)	59 (a)	60 (c)
61 (c)	62 (b)	63 (a)	64 (b)
65 (b)	66 (c)	67 (b)	68 (b)
69 (a)	70 (b)	71 (c)	72 (c)
73 (b)	74 (c)	75 (a)	

June 2013

LIBRARY & INFORMATION SCIENCE

Paper – II

(1) The distinct characteristic(s) of digital objects are
- (a) Physical Medium
- (b) Logical process
- (c) Conceptual recognition and transaction
- (d) All the above

(2) 'Who's who in India', an irregular publication is published by
- (a) Business Press, Bombay
- (b) Sterling, New Delhi
- (c) Tradesman & Men Asia, Delhi
- (d) Sahitya Samsad, Calcutta

(3) Which department of the Government of India deals with Public Libraries
- (a) Department of Archaeology
- (b) Department of Culture
- (c) Department of PrimaryEducation
- (d) Department of Science andTechnology

(4) Information on Prime Minister of Bangladesh can be found in
- (a) International Who's Who
- (b) Who's Who in Bangladesh
- (c) Current Biography
- (d) Statesman's Yearbook

(5) 'Eradication of Malaria in India 1990-1999' – a report can be categorized under

(a) Trend Report
(b) Review Report
(c) State of the Art Report
(d) Research Report

(6) Which is not a reprographic service ?

(a) Micro Copying (b) Paper Printing
(c) Blue Printing (d) Thermo Copying

(7) ERIC is sponsored by

(a) US National Health Institute
(b) Health and RehabilitationServices Division, A LA
(c) Department of Health Education & Welfare, Government of USA
(d) Health Science information Centre, USA

(8) In the library hierarchy which level of management is responsible for execution of policies ?

(a) Middle level (b) Operational level
(c) Top level (d) Lower level

(9) METS stands for

(a) Machine EncodedTransmission System
(b) Metadata Encoded for Textual Sources
(c) Machine Encoded Textual Standard
(d) Metadata EncodingTransmission Standard

(10) Sector Device is an extension of

(a) Gap Device (b) Empty Device
(c) Octave Device (d) Group Notation Device

(11) "Control, Disease, Malaria, Brain" indicates that it is

(a) Raw Title (b) Expressive Title
(c) Kernel Title (d) Transformed Title

(12) A graphical representation using symbols to represent operations, data, flow, etc. is

(a) Logical Chart (b) Flow Chart

(c) System Flow Chart (d) Network Chart

(13) The 12 rules for relational database were given by

(a) E.F. Codd (b) Charles Babbage

(c) James Weyer (d) Tim Berners Lee

(14) A technique displaying graphic information on screen, pixel by pixel with bits held in main memory is

(a) Bit handling (b) Bit mapping

(c) Bit pattern (d) Bit matrix

(15) ZOTERO is a ______.

(a) Content Management System

(b) Reference Management System

(c) Serials Management System

(d) Bibliographic RreferenceManagement System

(16) A network in which the host computer controls different nodes which further control other nodes, is known as

(a) Star Network

(b) Ring Network

(c) Hierarchical Network

(d) Multipoint Network

(17) Impact factor is devised by

(a) Eugene Garfield (b) Alan Pritchard

(c) David Hume (d) Louis Brandeis

(18) A skilful method of providing means, mechanism and structural elements to streamline organizational work is known as

(a) Role Analysis (b) Strategic Planning

(c) Work Culture (d) Autonomous Planning

(19) Financial allocation made to a library for purchase of furniture andequipments usually comes under the budget head

(a) Recurring grant (b) Endowments

(c) Non-recurring grant (d) Annual grant

(20) Historical/Government records related to an organisation are maintained in

(i) Archieves (ii) Museums

(iii) Repositories (iv) Government libraries

Codes :

(A) (i) and (ii) are correct

(B) (ii) and (iii) are correct.

(C) (i) and (iii) are correct.

(D) (ii) and (iv) are correct

(21) Major elements of a profession are

(i) Philosophy (ii) Body of knowledge

(iii) Publicity (iv) Status

Codes :

(A) (i), (ii), (iv) are correct

(B) (i), (ii), (iii) are correct

(C) (ii), (iii), (iv) are correct

(D) (i), (iii), (iv) are correct.

(22) Which of the following states don't have library legislation ?

(i) Haryana (ii) Delhi

(iii) J & K (iv) Manipur

Codes :

(A) (i) and (ii) are correct

(B) (ii) and (iii) are correct.

(C) (i) and (iv) are correct.

(D) (ii) and (iii) are correct.

(23) Which of the following principles are associated with library building planning ?

(i) Principle of Uniformity

(ii) Principle of Comfortability

(iii) Principle of Simplicity

(iv) Principle of Continuity

Codes :

(A) (i), (ii) and (iii) are correct.

(B) (ii), (iii) and (iv) are correct.

(C) (i), (ii) and (iv) are correct.

(D) (iii), (iv) and (i) are correct.

(24) ETD database in India is maintained by

(i) Shodhgangotri

(ii) Vidyanidhi

(iii) Shodhganga

(iv) INDEST-AICTE consortium

Codes :

(A) (i) and (iii) are correct

(B) (ii), (iii) and (iv) are correct.

(C) (ii) and (iii) are correct.

(D) (iii) and (iv) are correct

(25) Vocabulary in a database is controlled by

(i) Thesaurus files (ii) Dictionary files

(iii) Standard files (iv) Authority files

Codes :

(A) (i) and (ii) are correct.

(B) (iii) and (iv) are correct

(C) (i) and (iii) are correct.

(D) (i) and (iv) are correct

(26) Limitations of Bibliometrics is/are

(i) Analysing research and development trends

(ii) Describing text, not necessarily meaning and context
(iii) Identifying the active areas of research
(iv) Citation bias

Codes :

(A) (ii) and (iv) are correct.
(B) (i) and (iii) are correct.
(C) (i), (ii) and (iv) are correct.
(D) (ii) and (iii) are correct.

(27) Identify the technique(s) to collect the data regarding the number of persons visited the periodical section of the library at different hours of the day.

(i) Questionnaire (ii) Interview
(iii) Observation (iv) Library records

Codes :

(A) (i) and (ii) are correct.
(B) (ii) and (iii) are correct.
(C) (iii) and (iv) are correct.
(D) (ii) and (iv) are correct.

(28) Which of the following are prohibited under copyright ?

(i) Downloading a document, printing multiple copies
(ii) Placing a copyright protected document on web-server
(iii) Downloading a document and save it in folder
(iv) Downloading a document with license to use and E-mailing it

Codes :

(A) (i), (iii) and (iv) are correct.
(B) (i), (ii) and (iii) are correct.
(C) (iii), (iv) and (ii) are correct.
(D) (i), (ii) and (iv) are correct.

(29) The professional ethics help to ____.

(i) Get the right direction

(ii) Enhance image

(iii) Get more salaries

(iv) Resolve day to day issues

Codes :

(A) (ii) and (iii) are correct.

(B) (i) and (iv) are correct.

(C) (i) and (ii) are correct.

(D) (ii) and (iv) are correct.

(30) Match the following :

	List – I		List – II
(a)	Systematic Bibliography	(i)	List of macro/ micro ideas of articles
(b)	Analytical or Critical Bibliography	(ii)	Investigation of physical nature of books
(c)	Historical Bibliography	(iii)	Listing of items with minimum details
(d)	Documentary Bibliography	(iv)	Concerned with art of writing, printing and binding

Codes :	(a)	(b)	(c)	(d)
(A)	i	iv	iii	ii
(B)	ii	i	iv	iii
(C)	iii	ii	iv	i
(D)	ii	iv	iii	i

(31) Match the following queries with their appropriate category of reference source :

	List – I		List – II
(a)	Enrolment of students in auniversity	(i)	Yearbook

(b)	Weather of Denmark	(ii) Statistical Source
(c)	No. of foreigners visited World Book Fair in 2011	(iii) Directory
(d)	No. of hospitals in China	(iv) Geographical Source

Codes :	**(a)**	**(b)**	**(c)**	**(d)**
(A)	iv	iii	I	ii
(B)	i	iii	ii	iv
(C)	ii	iv	i	iii
(D)	iii	iv	i	ii

(32) Match the following :

	List – I	**List – II**
(a)	1st Law of Library Science	(i) Real time access
(b)	2nd Law of Library Science	(ii) Search engine & subject gateways
(c)	3rd Law of Library Science	(iii) Web access to resources
(d)	4th Law of Library Science	(iv) Open access initiatives

Codes :	**(a)**	**(b)**	**(c)**	**(d)**
(A)	iii	iv	ii	i
(B)	iv	i	ii	iii
(C)	i	iii	ii	iv
(D)	ii	iv	i	iii

(33) Match the following :

	List – I	**List – II**
(a)	Douglas McGregor	(i) Scientific Management School
(b)	Abraham Maslow	(ii) Theory of Authority Structure

(c) F.W. Taylor (iii) Self Actualisation Needs

(d) Max Weber (iv) Theory X and Theory Y

Codes :	**(a)**	**(b)**	**(c)**	**(d)**
(A)	iv	iii	I	ii
(B)	ii	iii	i	iv
(C)	iii	iv	ii	i
(D)	i	iv	ii	iii

(34) Match the following DDC numbers :

List – I	**List – II**
(a) Education	(i) 770
(b) Medicine	(ii) 370
(c) Photography	(iii) 610
(d) Astronomy	(iv) 520

Codes :	**(a)**	**(b)**	**(c)**	**(d)**
(A)	iii	i	iv	ii
(B)	ii	iii	i	iv
(C)	i	iv	iii	ii
(D)	iv	ii	i	iii

(35) Match the following :

List – I	**List – II**
(a) Key to a given collection	(i) Abstract
(b) Key to literary sources on a subject	(ii) Index
(c) Representation of subject concept	(iii) Catalogue
(d) Condensation of a document	(iv) Bibliography

Codes :	**(a)**	**(b)**	**(c)**	**(d)**
(A)	iii	iv	ii	i
(B)	ii	iii	iv	i
(C)	i	ii	iii	iv
(D)	iv	i	ii	iii

(36) Match the following :

	List – I		**List – II**
(a)	Unity of command	(i)	Specialization
(b)	Unity of direction	(ii)	Strength in unity
(c)	Esprit de corps	(iii)	Orders from only one person
(d)	Division of work	(iv)	One boss, one plan

Codes :	**(a)**	**(b)**	**(c)**	**(d)**
(A)	iv	iii	ii	i
(B)	ii	iv	iii	i
(C)	iii	iv	ii	i
(D)	i	iv	iii	ii

(37) Give in sequence, the following in order of their origin :

(i) National Library (ii) Calcutta Public Library

(iii) Imperial Library Act (iv) Imperial Library

Codes :

(A) ii iii iv i (B) i ii iii iv

(C) iii i iv ii (D) ii iv iii i

(38) Arrange the following according to year of publication :

(i) Colon Classification

(ii) Prolegomena to Classification

(iii) Five Laws of Library Science

(iv) Classified Catalogue Code

Codes :

(A) iii iv i ii (B) iv ii i iii

(C) iii i iv ii (D) i ii iv iii

(39) **Assertion (A) :** Digitization has proved to be possible for every format and medium held by library.

Reason (R) : All libraries are making their text and visual collections digitized.

Codes :

(A) (A) is true, but (R) is false

(B) (A) is false, but (R) is true.

(C) Both (A) and (R) are true.

(D) Both (A) and (R) are false.

(40) **Assertion (A) :** In spite of political, economic and technological support, the growth of Public Library System is lopsided.

Reason (R) : The public libraries are totally depending on cess/tax amounts.

Codes :

(A) Both (A) and (R) are true

(B) Both (A) and (R) are false

(C) (A) is true, but (R) is false

(D) (A) is false, but (R) is true.

(41) **Assertion (A) :** 'Pay and Use' concept has not been accepted in libraries of India.

Reason (R) : Library staff do not possess the essential skills required for product development and promotion.

Codes :

(A) Both (A) and (R) are true.

(B) (A) is true but (R) are false.

(C) (R) is true, but (A) is false.

(D) Both (A) and (R) are false

(42) **Assertion (A) :** Library Science profession in India enjoys the status at par with medical, legal and management professions.

Reason (R) : S.R. Ranganathan's contributions and teachings for Indian librarianship secured a status to the profession.

Codes :

(A) (A) is true, but (R) is false.

(B) (A) is false, but (R) is true.

(C) Both (A) and (R) are true

(D) Both (A) and (R) are false.

(43) **Assertion (A) :** In conducting research, Social Sciences are not considered at par with natural sciences.

Reason (R) : Research in Social Sciences can't be performed so rigorously as can be in Natural Sciences.

Codes :

(A) Both (A) and (R) are true.

(B) Both (A) and (R) are false.

(C) (A) is true, but (R) is false.

(D) (A) is false, but (R) is true.

(44) **Assertion (A) :** Research starts in mind first and then in laboratories.

Reason (R) : Systematically conducted research leads to generalization.

Codes :

(A) (A) is true, but (R) is false.

(B) (A) is false, but (R) is true.

(C) Both (A) and (R) are true.

(D) Both (A) and (R) are false.

(45) **Assertion (A) :** Systematic and efficient use of statistical tools in research helps in precise interpretation of research results.

Reason (R) : Statistical tools cannot give specific explanations of the data.

Codes :

(A) Both (A) and (R) are true

(B) (A) is true and (R) is false.

(C) Both (A) and (R) are false

(D) (A) is false and (R) is true.

(46) People are assigned into specific organization or groups in _______ approach.

(A) Top-down approach

(B) Down-top approach

(C) Top-bottom system approach

(D) Down-top system approach

(47) The basic feature(s) of social software is/are :

(A) Social interaction

(B) Personal interaction

(C) Enjoying social software

(D) (A) and (C) are correct.

(48) Authors of social media enjoy ______ of contents.

(A) Self created contents

(B) Contents from magazines

(C) Contents from many formats

(D) Contents from many languages

(49) The reason/s attributed to the popularity of social networking is/are :

(A) Masses have started using internet.

(B) All have free access to internet.

(C) All are technology literates

(D) Stimulation of on-linecommunities over the traditional communities

(50) The social software tools allow.

(A) Easy participation

(B) Quick networking

(C) Consumer networking

(D) Both (A) & (B)

ANSWERS

01 (d)	02 (a)	03 (b)	04 (d)
05 (a)	06 (c)	07 *	08 (a)
09 (d)	10 (c)	11 (c)	12 (b)
13 (a)	14 (b)	15 (d)	16 (c)
17 (a)	18 (b)	19 (c)	20 (c)
21 (a)	22 (b)	23 (b)	24 (c)
25 (b)	26 (a)	27 (c)	28 (d)
29 (c)	30 (c)	31 (d)	32 (a)
33 (a)	34 (b)	35 (a)	36 (a)
37 (d)	38 (c)	39 (a)	40 (c)
41 (a)	42 (b)	43 (a)	44 (c)
45 (a)	46 (a)	47 (d)	48 (a)
49 (a)	50 (d)		

Note : Q.No. 7 : No one is correct. ERIC sponsored by Institute of Education Science of United States Department of Education.

June 2013
LIBRARY AND INFORMATION SCIENCE
Paper – III

(1) "Poole's Index to Periodical Literature" was brought out by

(a) William Frederick (b) F.W. Lancaster

(c) Van Rijsbergen (d) H.P. Luhn

(2) Walford's Guide to Reference Material is published by

(a) American Library association, Chicago

(b) R.R. Bowkar, London

(c) Library Association Publishing, London

(d) Learned Information Ltd., New Jersey

(3) Starting, Chaining, Browsing, Differentiating, Monitoring, Extracting, Verification and Ending are important stages of which information seeking behavior model ?

(a) Dervin's Model (b) Ellis Model

(c) Marchionnini Model (d) Kuhlthan Model

(4) What kind of arrangement is followed in LISA ?

(a) Alphabetical (b) Chronological

(c) Classified (d) Geographical

(5) Webform is used in

(a) Synchronous Virtual Reference Service

(b) Asynchronous Virtual Reference Service

(c) Both (A) & (B)

(d) None of the above

(6) An online search in which all aspects of the records in natural language may be used as sought terms is

(a) Alphabetical collateral search

(b) Multi-aspect search

(c) Free text searching

(d) Streaming search

(7) Science Abstracts published by

(a) INSPEC (Institute of Electrical Engineering)

(b) Institute of Physics, London

(c) American Institute of Physics

(d) PSOJ (Physical Society ofJapan)

(8) Work study, standardised tools, selecting and training of workers are the contributions of

(a) Louis Brndeis (b) F.W. Taylor

(c) Henry Fayol (d) Lyndall Urwick

(9) When the population is heterogenous, which of the following methods give better results ?

(a) Purposive Sampling (b) Quota Sampling

(c) Random Sampling (d) Stratified Random Sampling

(10) Which of the following is/are not database object

(a) Tables (b) Queries

(c) Relationships (d) Re-

(11) What is the process of transferring software programme from secondary storage media to the hard disc called ?

(a) Download (b) Upload

(c) Installation (d) Storage

(12) Name a technique used for searching sorted data in a database

(a) Boolean operator (b) Inverting file

(c) Indexing (d) Binary

(13) Information about Government of India's stand on 'FDI' can be found In

(a) Gazetteer of India

(b) Britanniea Book of the Year

(c) Statesman's Yearbook

(d) Asian Recorder

(14) "Anomalous State of Knowledge (ASK) Model", one of the user centered models of information retrieval was proposed by

(a) P. Ingwersen (b) T. Saracevic

(c) J.N. Belkin (d) D. Ellis

(15) The 'Cranefield Test', associated with evaluation of information retrieval system was carried under the direction of ______.

(a) C.W. Cleverdon

(b) G. Salton

(c) D.C. Blair & M.E. Maron

(d) E. Voorhees

(16) LAMP stands for

(a) Library Archives Management Programme

(b) Laser Analysis and Multimedia Performance

(c) Linux Apache.MySQL Perl

(d) Library Automation Management Protocol

(17) "Information Literacy Competency Standards for Higher Education" is prepared by

(a) AASL (b) IFLA

(c) SCONUL (d) ACRL

(18) Name the storage medium (compatible with speed of CPU) forstoring instructions or data temporarily during processing

(a) RAM (b) ROM

(c) Cache (d) EPROM

(19) "Scitation" is the online host service of

(a) American Institute of Physics

(b) University of Maryland

(c) Society for Industrial Research

(d) Oxford University (D)

(20) The process of surrogation, repackaging and compaction of the primary literature that results in creation of secondary journals, is

(a) Newsletter

(b) Abstracting and IndexingPeriodical

(c) House Journals

(d) Electronic Journal

(21) Which of the following is not a language of DBMS ?

(a) DDL (b) DML

(c) PASCAL (d) PLI

(22) How do we render the name 'Bernardo Augustine De Voto' ?

(a) Voto, Bernardo, Augustine De

(b) De Voto, Augustine, Bernardo

(c) Bernardo Augustine, De Voto

(d) Electronic Journal

(23) Which reference tool defines Reference service as ".... that phase of work which is directly concerned

with assistance to readers in securing information and in using the resources of the library in study and research" ?

(A) Encyclopaedia of Librarianship

(B) Encyclopaedia of Library and Information Science

(C) ALA Glossary of Library Terms

(D) ALA World Encyclopaedia ofLibrary & Information Services

(24) Indian National Advisory Board for Libraries was setup in 1966 by

(A) Association of IndianUniversities

(B) Ministry of Education

(C) Planning Commission

(D) University Grants Commission

(25) The process of establishing headings and providing 'Cross references' is called

(A) Access points (B) Headings

(C) Authority control (D) Bibliographic Records

(26) Which set of rules is applicable for exchange of files over Internet ?

(A) FTP/IP (B) HTTP

(C) HTML (D) HYPERLINK

(27) The first printed works are called

(A) Impensis (B) Incunabula

(C) Impression (D) Imprimatur

(28) Which Law of Library Science, restated with emphasis on information as a dynamic, continuum and never ending phenomenon ?

(A) Fifth Law (B) Fourth Law

(C) Third Law (D) Second Law

(29) Andrew Carnegie donated two million pounds for development of ______.

(A) Library Collection (B) Library Building

(C) Library Furniture (D) Library Staff

(30) Whose model of communication of knowledge suggests that communication as an open system may be regarded as subjective, selective, variable and yet unpredictable ?

(A) G Gerbner

(B) Juger Hebermans

(C) Shanon & Weaver

(D) M. Foucault

(31) Which Committee/Commission recommended that Imperial Librarybe designated as Copyright Library?

(A) Fayzee Commission, 1939

(B) Riche Committee, 1926

(C) Statham Committee, 1932

(D) Sadler Committee, 1916

(32) What are the four entities of FRBR model ?

(A) Personality, Matter, Energy, Space

(B) Books, Form, Availability,Type

(C) Work, Expression, Manifestation, Item

(D) Discipline, Entity, Action,Personality

(33) Who said that information is both a product and process ?

(A) S.R. Ranganathan (B) J. Martin

(C) D.J. Foskett (D) S.C. Bradford

(34) The process of planning, allocating, organizing and evaluating library tasks and activities within the framework of major objectives, mission and policy refers to

(A) Functional control

(B) Functional Classification

(C) Functional Approach

(D) Functional Authority

(35) One of the authorized user makes bulk downloading of a Journal using robots and consequently licensor blocks access of the journal. What may be the most appropriate action(s) that librarian should initiate?

(i) Cancellation of authentication of the said user.

(ii) Asking the licensor for blocking up the access without prior information.

(iii) Investigate and take corrective measures.

(iv) Notify user community of user restrictions.

Codes:

(A) (ii), (iv) are correct. (B) (ii), (iii) are correct.

(C) (i), (iii) are correct. (D) (i), (ii) are correct.

(36) The purposes of Metadata are

(i) Unique identification

(ii) Authentication of records

(iii) Shelf arrangement

(iv) Shows the collection of a library

Codes:

(A) (i), (ii) are correct. (B) (ii), (iii) are correct.

(C) (iii), (iv) are correct. (D) (iv), (i) are correct.

(37) The primary difference between knowledge classification and library classification are

(i) Knowledge classification arranges knowledge itself.

(ii) Library classification arranges the expression of knowledge in the form of documents.

(iii) Knowledge classification is the basis of Library Classification.

(iv) Knowledge classification follows system of numbers, called notation.

Codes:

(A) (i) and (ii) are correct.

(B) (ii) and (iii) are correct.

(C) (i), (ii) and (iv) are correct.

(D) (i), (ii) and (iii) are correct

(38) Which of the following activities are supported by UGC ?

(i) Facilitating increased access to information.

(ii) Monitoring the implementationof revised curriculum.

(iii) Making policies for human resource development.

(iv) Funding all academic libraries.

Codes:

(A) (i) and (ii) are correct.

(B) (i) and (iii) are correct.

(C) (ii) and (iii) are correct.

(D) (i) and (iv) are correct.

(39) Which of the following methods are suitable to achieve quality of teaching, learning in LIS ?

(i) Research-lcd teaching

(ii) State of the art computer lab

(iii) Problem-based learning

(iv) Introducing the course at degree level

Codes:

(A) (ii) and (iv) (B) (i), (iii) and (iv)

(C) (i) and (iii) (D) (iii) and (iv)

(40) Poor 'Accessibility' and less 'affordability' of journal subscription in print era led to

(i) High allocation of funds for serials

(ii) Open access movement

(iii) Decrease in subscription of journals

(iv) E-journal consortia subscription

Codes:

(A) (i) & (ii) are correct. (B) (i), (ii), (iv) are correct.

(C) (ii), (iv) are correct. (D) (i), (ii), (iii) are correct.

(41) The alternatives and modifications to H-Index are

(i) I-index

(ii) Pure-h Index

(iii) Scimgo Journal Rank

(iv) European Impact Factor

Codes:

(A) (i) & (iii) are correct.

(B) (i) & (ii) are correct.

(C) (i) and (iv) are correct.

(D) (ii) & (iii) are correct.

(42) Digitization of various cultural resources is possible through

(i) Scanners

(ii) Digital cameras

(iii) Video cameras

(iv) Smart & Mobile phones

Codes:

(A) (i), (ii) are correct.

(B) (iv), (iii) are correct.

(C) (iii), (iv) are correct.

(D) (i), (ii), (iii) & (iv) are correct.

(43) What is/are not common feature/s between RFID & Barcode Technology ?

(i) Read more than one item at a time

(ii) Able to locate specific items on shelves

(iii) Programmable

(iv) Read while item is moving

Codes:

(A) (i), (ii) are correct.

(B) (iii), (iv) are correct.

(C) (ii), (iv) are correct.

(D) All the above are correct

(44) When a librarian has to show the rationale for the purchase of more e-resources, which of the following/s will help to support his/her stand ?

(i) Collection development policy

(ii) Indent from users

(iii) Book selection tools

(iv) All the above

Codes:

(A) (i) and (ii) are correct.

(B) (i) and (iii) are correct.

(C) (ii) and (iii) are correct.

(D) (iv) is correct.

(45) **Assertion (A) :** Machine translation is not a fully dependable service.

Reason (R) : The semantics of languages are not fully encoded in algorithms.

Codes :

(A) (A) is true, but (R) is false.

(B) Both (A) & (R) are true.

(C) (A) is false, but (R) is true.

(D) Both (A) & (R) are false.

(46) Match the following :

	List – I	List – II
(a)	INFLIB NET	(i) Digital Library
(b)	INDEST AICTE	(ii) Resource aggregator
(c)	DELNET	(iii) E-consortia
(d)	e-Gyankosh	(iv) Organisation

Codes :	(a)	(b)	(c)	(d)
(A)	i	ii	iii	iv
(B)	iv	iii	ii	i
(C)	iii	ii	i	iv
(D)	ii	iii	iv	i

(47) Match the following :

	List – I		List – II
(a)	Amenable to further algebraic treatment	(i)	Mean deviation
(b)	Estimated without knowing values of extreme items	(ii)	Median
(c)	Mathematieally and logically incorrect	(iii)	Inter-quartile deviation
(d)	The dispersion does not cover all items of a series	(iv)	Arithmetic means

Codes :	(a)	(b)	(c)	(d)
(A)	iv	ii	i	iii
(B)	iii	ii	i	iv
(C)	ii	iv	iii	i
(D)	i	iii	iv	ii

(48) Match the following :

	List – I		List – II
(a)	Trade Publisher	(i)	American
(b)	Subject book publisher	(ii)	Psychological Society
(c)	Government Press	(iii)	Harper Collins
(d)	Scholarly Publisher	(iv)	W.B. Saunders

Codes :	(a)	(b)	(c)	(d)
(A)	ii	iv	iii	i
(B)	iv	iii	i	ii

(C)	i	iv	iii	ii
(D)	iii	iv	i	ii

(49) Match the following :

	List – I		List – II
(a)	Statistical Quality/ ProcessControl (SQC/SPC)	(i)	Identify the intensity of each problem in the productionprocess
(b)	Check Sheets	(ii)	Selected variables checked
(c)	Pareto Chart	(iii)	Identify the Relationship between problems and causes
(d)	Fish Bone Diagram	(iv)	Record variables in the production process

Codes :	**(a)**	**(b)**	**(c)**	**(d)**
(A)	ii	iv	i	iii
(B)	v	ii	iii	i
(C)	iii	iv	i	ii
(D)	i	ii	iv	iii

(50) Match the following :

	List – I		List– II
(a)	Sinha Committee	(i)	Library staff strength
(b)	Dr. S.R. Ranganathan Committee	(ii)	Central Medical Library
(c)	Report of Dr. Shaw and Dr. D.B Krishna Rao	(iii)	Libraries at Panchayat, Block, District and State level
(d)	Dr. J. Bhore Committee	(iv)	National Agricultural System of Agriculture Libraries

Codes :	**(a)**	**(b)**	**(c)**	**(d)**
(A)	iii	i	ii	iv
(B)	iv	iii	ii	i
(C)	iii	i	iv	ii
(D)	i	iii	ii	iv

(51) Match the following :

	List – I		**List– II**
(a)	Finding solution to the problem of pilferage in libraries	(i)	Historical Research
(b)	Implementation of cloud computing services in special libraries	(ii)	Action Research
(c)	A study of Mathematician turned librarian	(iii)	Experimental Research
(d)	Use of web resources in Central Universities of India	(iv)	Survey Research

Codes :	**(a)**	**(b)**	**(c)**	**(d)**
(A)	ii	iii	i	iv
(B)	iii	ii	iv	i
(C)	iv	i	ii	iii
(D)	i	iv	iii	ii

(52) Match the following :

	List – I		**List– II**
(a)	Internal Files	(i)	WPD
(b)	Universal File Format	(ii)	OeB
(c)	Corel's Word Perfect	(iii)	HTML
(d)	Microsoft Reader	(iv)	RTF

Codes :	(a)	(b)	(c)	(d)
(A)	i	iii	ii	iv
(B)	ii	iv	iii	i
(C)	iv	ii	i	iii
(D)	iii	iv	i	ii

(53) Match the following :

	List – I		List– II
(a)	Classical Models	(i)	Ruesch and Bateson's Functional Model
(b)	Linear Model	(ii)	Aristotle
(c)	Non-linear Model	(iii)	Lasswell
(d)	Multi dimensional	(iv)	Westley and Mackan's Conceptual Model

Codes :	(a)	(b)	(c)	(d)
(A)	ii	iii	iv	i
(B)	ii	iv	i	iii
(C)	i	ii	iii	iv
(D)	iii	ii	iv	i

(54) Match the following :

	List – I		List– II
(a)	Henri La Fontaine	(i)	Expansive Classification
(b)	H.E. Bliss	(ii)	Bibliographic Classification
(c)	C.A. Cutter	(iii)	LC
(d)	J.C.M. Hansar	(iv)	UDC

Codes :	(a)	(b)	(c)	(d)
(A)	iv	ii	i	iii
(B)	iii	ii	iv	i
(C)	ii	iv	i	iii
(D)	i	iii	ii	iv

(55) Match the following:

List – I	**List– II**
(a) PDFA	(i) High colour depth images
(b) HTML	(ii) Rules for Encoding documents electronically
(c) TIFF	(iii) File format for long term archiving
(d) XML	(iv) Language for web pages

Codes :	**(a)**	**(b)**	**(c)**	**(d)**
(A)	ii	iii	i	iv
(B)	iii	iv	i	ii
(C)	i	iii	ii	iv
(D)	iv	ii	iii	i

(56) Match the books against their authors :

List – I	**List– II**
(a) Introduction to Modern Information Retrieval (McGraw Hill)	(i) H. Borko & C. Bernier
(b) Indexing Concepts and Methods (Academic Press)	(ii) G. Salton & M.J. McGill
(c) Thesaurus Construction : A Practical Manual (Aslib)	(iii) J.E. Rowley & R. Hartley
(d) Organising Knowledge : An Introduction to Managing Access to Information (Ashgate)	(iv) J. Aitchison & A. Gilchrist

Codes :	**(a)**	**(b)**	**(c)**	**(d)**
(A)	i	ii	iii	iv
(B)	ii	i	iv	iii
(C)	iv	i	ii	iii
(D)	iii	i	iv	ii

(57) Match the following :

List – I	List– II
(a) Papyrus	(i) Assyria & Babylonia
(b) Handmade paper	(ii) Egypt
(c) Clay tablets	(iii) Medieval Europe
(d) Vellum/ Parchment	(iv) China

Codes :	(a)	(b)	(c)	(d)
(A)	ii	iv	i	iii
(B)	iv	ii	iii	i
(C)	iii	iv	i	ii
(D)	iii	ii	iv	i

(58) Match the following :

List – I	List– II
(a) Icon	(i) Character strings
(b) Menus	(ii) Select objects on the screen
(c) Dialogue Bou	(iii) Bit mapped region
(d) Pointing devices	(iv) Obtain information from the end users

Codes :	(a)	(b)	(c)	(d)
(A)	i	ii	iii	iv
(B)	iii	iv	ii	i
(C)	ii	iii	iv	i
(D)	iii	i	iv	ii

(59) Match the following :

List – I	List– II
(a) Resource Description	(i) MARC
(b) Resource Discovery	(ii) ISO 10160/ 10161
(c) Resource Exchange	(iii) Dublin Care
(d) Interlibrary Loan	(iv) Z 39.50

Codes :	**(a)**	**(b)**	**(c)**	**(d)**
(A)	ii	i	iv	iii
(B)	iv	ii	i	iii
(C)	iii	iv	ii	i
(D)	iii	iv	i	ii

(60) Match the following :

	List – I		**List– II**
(a)	Public Library Extension	(i)	KD Metcalf
(b)	Academic Library Management	(ii)	M A Gelfand
(c)	University Libraries for Developing Countries	(iii)	L R McColvin
(d)	Planning Academic and Research Library Buildings	(iv)	M B Line

Codes :	**(a)**	**(b)**	**(c)**	**(d)**
(A)	iii	iv	ii	i
(B)	iv	ii	i	iii
(C)	iii	i	iv	ii
(D)	ii	iii	i	iv

(61) Match the following :

	List – I		**List– II**
(a)	Indian Cultural Heritage	(i)	TKDL
(b)	Race & Brittle documents	(ii)	IGNCA
(c)	Traditional Knowledge	(iii)	C-DAC
(d)	Mobile Digital Library	(iv)	National Library

Codes :	(a)	(b)	(c)	(d)
(A)	i	iv	iii	ii
(B)	iv	iii	ii	i
(C)	ii	iv	i	iii
(D)	iii	ii	iv	i

(62) Match the following :

List – I	List– II
(a) Carol Kuhlthau	(i) 8 stages
(b) David Ellis	(ii) ISB is a 6 stage process
(c) M.J. Belkin	(iii) ISB is of 8 key activities
(d) Marchionnini	(iv) ISB is 4 Dimension characteristic

Codes :	(a)	(b)	(c)	(d)
(A)	ii	iii	iv	i
(B)	ii	iii	i	iv
(C)	iii	i	iv	ii
(D)	iv	ii	i	iii

(63) **Assertion (A) :** Colon classification is popular in online catalogues.

Reason (R) : Traditional classification systems are used in online searching advantageously.

Codes :

(a) (A) is true, but (R) is false.

(b) Both (A) & (R) are true, but(R) is not the correct explanation of (A).

(c) (A) is false, but (R) is true.

(d) Both (A) & (R) are true.

(64) **Assertion (A) :** Technical writing standards, style manuals and citation standards are very essential in structuring the research report.

Reason (R) : Value will get enhanced by standardising the structure of research report.

Codes:

(a) (A) is true and (R) is partially

(b) Both (A) and (R) are true.

(c) Both (A) and (R) are false.

(d) (A) is true and (R) is false.

(65) **Assertion (A) :** The encouraging environment of all time, full reading halls with the students in the libraries is diminishing day by day.

Reason (R) : All the reading material is easily available and accessible on Internet to all the students.

Codes :

(a) Both (A) and (R) are true.

(b) Both (A) and (R) are false.

(c) (A) is true, but (R) is false.

(d) (A) is false, but (R) is true

(66) **Assertion (A) :** There is a tremendous increase in number of doctoral degrees being awarded in library and information science.

Reason (R) : Any academician in LIS holding a Ph.D degree is entitled to supervise research programme.

Codes :

(a) (A) is true and (R) is partially

(b) Both (A) and (R) are true.

(c) Both (A) and (R) are false.

(d) (A) is false and (R) is true.

(67) **Assertion (A) :** The information seeking behaviour research at the current times is on the social and cultural context of human interaction with information.

Reason (R) : Attempt is being made to interpret social and cultural experiences of individuals with respect to their information seeking and searching experiences.

Codes :

(a) (A) is true and (R) is false.

(b) Both (A) and (R) are false.

(c) (A) is false and (R) is true.

(d) Both (A) and (R) are true.

(68) **Assertion (A) :** With the emergence of Internet, there is no need for reference service in this technology-based era.

Reason (R) : Internet has allowed access to every one to seek his/her information from anywhere, any time.

Codes :

(a) Both (A) and (R) are true.

(b) Both (A) and (R) are false.

(c) (A) is false but (R) is partiallytrue.

(d) (A) is true, but (R) is false.

(69) **Assertion (A) :** Micrographic services have lost acceptance for preservation and dissemination of archival matcrial.

Reason (R) : ICT has brought in cost effective alternatives and replaced micrographic services.

Codes :

(a) (A) is true and (R) is partially- true.

(b) Both (A) & (R) are false.

(c) (A) is true, (R) is false.

(d) (A) is false, (R) is true.

(70) **Assertion (A) :** Institutions generate information through research and development activities.

Reason (R) : All such generated information forms the grey literature.

Codes :

(a) Both (A) and (R) are false.

(b) (A) is true, (R) is partially true

(c) (A) is false, (R) is true.

(d) Both (A) and (R) are true.

(71) **Assertion (A) :** Maximizing the access to information in higher education is the motto of UGC-INFONET Project.

Reason (R) : The financial grants of UGC-INFONET are not being fully utilized by all University Libraries for the assigned purpose.

Codes :

(a) Both (A) and (R) are false.

(b) (A) is true and (R) is partiallytrue.

(c) (A) is true and (R) is false.

(d) (A) is false and (R) is true.

(72) **Assertion (A) :** The effective reprographic service in libraries indirectly demotivates the user for tearing/theft of reading material.

Reason (R) : The user gets the photocopy of reading materials free of cost.

Codes :

(a) (A) is false and (R) is true.

(b) Both (A) and (R) are true.

(c) (A) is true and (R) is false.

(d) Both (A) and (R) are false

(73) **Assertion (A) :** RFID technology is still not widely installed in Indian Library Environment.

Reason (R) : The standardization, application and innovation are constantly changing.

Codes :

(a) Both (A) & (R) are true and (R) is the correct explanation of (A).

(b) Both (A) & (R) are true, but (R) is not the correct explanation of

(c) (A) is true, but (R) is false.

(d) (A) is false, but (R) is true.

(74) **Assertion (A) :** Gap device is a non scientific solution to the problem of growing universe.

Reason (R) : A classificationist cannot forecast the areas/ subjects wherein some new ones may emerge.

Codes :

(a) (A) and (R) are true.

(b) (A) is true and (R) is false

(c) (A) is false and (R) is true.

(d) (A) and (R) are false.

(75) **Assertion (A) :** All the states in India have enacted library legislation.

Reason (R) : NKC recommends for the enactment of library legislation in all the states.

Codes :

(a) Both (A) and (R) are true.

(b) Both (A) and (R) are false.

(c) (A) is true, but (R) is false.

(d) (A) is false, but (R) is true

ANSWERS

1 (a)	2 (c)	3 (b)	4 (c)
5 (b)	6 (c)	7 (a)	8 (b)
9 (d)	10 (c)	11 (c)	12 (d)
13 (d)	14 (c)	15 (a)	16 (c)
17 (d)	18 (c)	19 (a)	20 (b)
21 See Note	22 (d)	23 (c)	24 (b)
25 (c)	26 (b)	27 (b)	28 (a)
29 (b)	30 (a)	31 (b)	32 (c)
33 (b)	34 (c)	35 (d)	36 (a)
37 (d)	38 (b)	39 (c)	40 (c)

41 (b)	42 (d)	43 See Note	44 (a)
45 (b)	46 (b)	47 (a)	48 (d)
49 (a)	50 (c)	51 (a)	52 (d)
53 (a)	54 (a)	55 (b)	56 (b)
57 (a)	58 (d)	59 (d)	60 (a)
61 (c)	62 (a)	63 (c)	64 (a)
65 (c)	66 (a)	67 (d)	68 (c)
69 (a)	70 (c)	71 (b)	72 (c)
73 (b)	74 (a)	75 (d)	

Note : *Q. No. 21* **:** No one is Correct.

Q. No. 43 **:** The statement I & IV should be correct, that is not given in any option.

December 2013
LIBRARY & INFORMATION SCIENCE
Paper – II

(1) Name the scientist who said that Information Science is cluster of many disciplines where in the central core is 'Information'.

(a) B.C. Brooks (b) Fritz Machlup

(c) Daniel Bell (d) N.J. Belkin

(2) Which committee recommended that imperial library be designated as copyright library?

(a) Fayzee Committee, 1939

(b) Richey Committee, 1926

(c) Statham Committee, 1932

(d) Sadler Committee, 1916

(3) Who was the first Librarian of Imperial Library, Calcutta?

(a) John MacFarlane (b) Harinath De

(c) B.S. Kesavan (d) S.R. Ranghanathan

(4) Who coined the phrase 'Information Retrieval'?

(a) Calvin Mooers (b) S.R. Ranganathan

(c) J.D. Brown (d) H.P. Luhan

(5) In colon classification which indicator has been used for indicating interpolation?

(a) Comma (b) Hyphen

(c) Astericks (d) Ampersand

(6) What is Denudation?

(a) Is dividing classes to decrease the extension.

(b) Is dividing classes to increase the extension.

(c) Is dividing classes to increase intension and decrease extension.

(d) Is dividing classes to decrease intension.

(7) The International Body that coordinates the assignment of unique domain names, protocol address in

(a) IGF (b) IANA

(c) ICANN (d) ISP

(8) Name the Indian Librarian who was honoured with the title of "Knan Bahadur" in 1935 by the British Government.

(a) S.R. Ranganathan (b) B.S. Kesavan

(c) K.M. Asadullah (d) D.R. Kalia

(9) Which approach of information is not given by Wersig and Neveling?

(a) Structural Approach (b) Knowledge Approach

(c) Meaning Approach (d) Technique Approach

(10) Which of the following citation style manuals are from the same publisher?

(i) A.P.A. (ii) Turabian

(iii) Chicago (iv) M.L.A.

Codes :

(A) (i) and (ii) are correct

(B) (ii) and (iii) are correct.

(C) (iii) and (iv) are correct.

(D) (ii) and (iv) are correct

(11) Pre co-ordinate Indexing system perceives:

(i) Syntax (ii) Semantic

(iii) Context (iv) Relation

Codes :

(A) (i) and (iv) are correct

(B) (i) (ii) and (iv) are correct.

(C) (ii) (iii) and (iv) are correct.

(D) (ii) and (iv) are correct

(12) An indispensable function of Thesaurus is to

(i) Knowledge Classification

(ii) Grouping the words together according to similarity of meaning

(iii) Representation of Relationship between concepts

(iv) Knowledge Engineering

Codes :

(A) (i) and (ii) are correct

(B) (ii) and (iii) are correct.

(C) (iii) and (iv) are correct.

(D) (i) and (iv) are correct

(13) Which of the following are the basic components of expert system?

(i) User interface

(ii) Knowledge base

(iii) Inference Mechanism

(iv) Schema

Codes :

(A) (i), (ii) and (iii) (B) (ii), (iii) and (iv).

(C) (iii) (iv) and (i) (D) (iv), (iii) and (ii)

(14) Which of the following are the types factors studies under ANOVA

(i) Fixed (ii) Frequency
(iii) Calculated (iv) Random

Codes :

(A) (ii) and (iii) are correct
(B) (i) and (iv) are correct.
(C) (i) and (iii) are correct.
(D) (ii) and (iv) are correct

(15) Which of the following are the models of communication?

(i) Economic Theory Model
(ii) Stock Adjustment Model
(iii) Shanon Weaver Model
(iv) Schramm Model

Codes :

(A) (iii) and (iv) are correct
(B) (ii) and (iii) are correct.
(C) (i) and (ii) are correct.
(D) (ii) and (iv) are correct

(16) Which of the following are criteria for Web evaluation?

(i) Revision (ii) Response time
(iii) Format (iv) Archiving facility

Codes :

(A) (i) and (ii) are correct
(B) (ii) and (iv) are correct.
(C) (i) and (iii) are correct.
(D) (ii) and (iii) are correct

(17) Which of the following countries do not have a code of Ethics for library profession?

(i) America (ii) Sri Lanka
(iii) India (iv) China

Codes :

(A) (i) and (ii) are correct

(B) (i) and (iv) are correct.

(C) (iii) and (ii) are correct.

(D) (iii) and (iv) are correct

(18) Which of the following are the components of Search Engine?

(i) Spider (ii) TCP/IP

(iii) Search Mechanism (iv) Index

Codes :

(A) (iv), (i) and (ii) (B) (iii), (ii) and (i).

(C) (i) (iii) and (iv) (D) (ii), (iv) and (iii)

(19) When the permission of copyright owner is not needed?

(i) Criticism or review (ii) Translation

(iii) Research purpose (iv) Photocopy for sale

Codes :

(A) (i) and (iii) are correct

(B) (i) and (iv) are correct.

(C) (iii) and (iv) are correct.

(D) (ii) and (iii) are correct

(20) Which of the following are Library net works?

(i) Internet (ii) Indonet

(iii) INFLIBNET (iv) OCLC

Codes :

(A) (i) and (ii) are correct

(B) (ii) and (iv) are correct.

(C) (iii) and (iv) are correct.

(D) (i) and (iv) are correct

(21) Arrange the following University Libraries according to the year of their establishment:

(i) Madras University Library

(ii) Delhi University Library

(iii) Calcutta University Library

(iv) Bombay University Library

Codes :

(A) (iv) (ii) (iii) (i) (B) (ii) (i) (iv) (iii)

(C) (i) (iii) (ii) (iv) (D) (iii) (iv) (i) (ii)

(22) What is the correct sequence of the following sections of the main entry as per classified catalogue code (CCC)?

(i) Note Section (ii) Leading Section

(iii) Heading Section (iv) Title Section

Codes :

(A) (i) (iv) (iii) (ii) (B) (ii) (iii) (iv) (i)

(C) (iii) (iv) (ii) (i) (D) ((iv) (i) (iii) (ii)

(23) Arrange the following indexing sources according to the year of their first publication:

(i) Biological Abstracts (ii) Chemical Abstracts

(iii) Index Medicus

(iv) Poole's Index to Periodical Literature

Codes :

(A) (i) (ii) (iii) (iv) (B) (iv) (iii) (ii) (i)

(C) (iv) (ii) (iv) (iii) (D) (i) (iv) (iii) (ii)

(24) Arrange the following library associations according the their year of emergence:

(i) CILIP (ii) ALA

(iii) SLA (iv) ASLIB

Codes :

(A) (iii) (iv) (i) (ii) (B) (iii) (iv) (ii) (i)

(C) (ii) (iii) (iv) (i) (D) (ii) (iv) (i) (iii)

(25) Match the following:

	List – I	**List – II**
(a)	Library Advisory Committee	(i) 1962
(b)	Review Committee	(ii) 1963
(c)	DRTC	(iii) 1957
(d)	Sarada Ranganathan Endowned	(iv) 1961

Codes :	**(a)**	**(b)**	**(c)**	**(d)**
(A)	iv	iii	ii	i
(B)	iii	iv	i	ii
(C)	iii	i	iii	iv
(D)	i	iv	iii	ii

(26) Match the following:

	List – I	**List – II**
(a)	Facts on File	(i) Periodical Directory
(b)	World of Learning	(ii) Index
(c)	Concordance	(iii) Newspaper Digest
(d)	Willing's Press Guide	(iv) Directory

Codes :	**(a)**	**(b)**	**(c)**	**(d)**
(A)	i	iii	iv	ii
(B)	ii	i	iii	iv
(C)	iii	iv	ii	i
(D)	iv	ii	i	iii

(27) Match the following:

	List – I	**List – II**
(a)	McGroger Theory X	(i) Less External Control
(b)	McGroger Theory Y	(ii) PERT
(c)	Unity of Command	(iii) Workers' Participation in Decision Makeng
(d)	Time and Cost	(iv) All Powers in One Person

Codes :	(a)	(b)	(c)	(d)
(A)	iii	i	iv	ii
(B)	iv	i	iii	ii
(C)	ii	iv	iii	i
(D)	i	iii	ii	iv

(28) Match the following:

	List – I		List – II
(a)	User Education	(i)	James I Wyer
(b)	Conservative, Liberal and Moderate Theory of Reference Service	(ii)	Patricia B. knapp
(c)	Minimum, Middling and Maximum Theories of Reference Service	(iii)	Eugene P. Sheehy
(d)	Guide to Reference Book	(iv)	Samuel Rothstein

Codes :	(a)	(b)	(c)	(d)
(A)	ii	i	iv	iii
(B)	i	ii	iv	iii
(C)	iii	ii	iv	i
(D)	iv	iii	i	ii

(29) Match the following:

	List – I		List – II
(a)	W. Edward Deming	(i)	Quality Control Circles
(b)	Joseph M. Juran	(ii)	TQM
(c)	Armand V. Feigenbaum	(iii)	Planning Control, Improvement
(d)	Kaoru Ishikava	(iv)	Plan, Do, Check, Atc (PDCA)

Codes :	**(a)**	**(b)**	**(c)**	**(d)**
(A)	ii	iii	iv	i
(B)	iv	ii	i	iii
(C)	iii	iv	i	ii
(D)	iv	iii	ii	i

(30) Match the following:

	List – I		**List – II**
(a)	Encyclopaedia of Associations	(i)	Secondary sources
(b)	Whitaker's Almanac	(ii)	Primary sources
(c)	LISA	(iii)	Directories
(d)	Economic Times	(iv)	Yearbooks

Codes :	**(a)**	**(b)**	**(c)**	**(d)**
(A)	iii	iv	i	ii
(B)	iv	iii	i	ii
(C)	ii	i	iv	iii
(D)	i	iv	iii	ii

(31) Match the following:

	List – I		**List – II**
(a)	Books in Print	(i)	National Bibliography
(b)	Social Science: A Bibliography of Doctoral Dissertations	(ii)	Trade Bibliography
(c)	Asian Social Science Bibliography	(iii)	National & Trade Bibliography
(d)	Cumulative Book Index	(iv)	Subject Bibliography

Codes :	**(a)**	**(b)**	**(c)**	**(d)**
(A)	ii	i	iv	iii
(B)	i	iii	ii	iv
(C)	iv	i	ii	iii
(D)	iii	ii	i	iv

(32) Match the following:

	List – I		List – II
(a)	Dictionary	(i)	Foreign Language
(b)	Glossary	(ii)	Synonymous terms
(c)	Thesaurus	(iii)	Words, Synonyms
(d)	Lexicon	(iv)	Specific subjects

Codes :	(a)	(b)	(c)	(d)
(A)	iii	iv	ii	i
(B)	iv	iii	i	ii
(C)	i	ii	iv	iii
(D)	ii	iv	iii	i

(33) Match the following:

	List – I		List – II
(a)	Curriculum Development Committee (P.N. Kaula)	(i)	2001
(b)	Curriculum Development Committee (C.R. Karrisidappa)	(ii)	1992
(c)	Working Group on Libraries	(iii)	1910
(d)	Library Movement in Baroda	(iv)	1964

Codes :	(a)	(b)	(c)	(d)
(A)	ii	i	iv	iii
(B)	i	ii	iv	iii
(C)	iv	ii	iii	i
(D)	iii	iv	ii	i

(34) Match the following:

	List – I		List – II
(a)	Current Biography	(i)	Russia
(b)	Index Translationum	(ii)	University of Illinois
(c)	VINITI	(iii)	U.S.A.
(d)	Library Trends	(iv)	UNESCO

Codes :	**(a)**	**(b)**	**(c)**	**(d)**
(A)	iii	iv	i	ii
(B)	iv	i	ii	iii
(C)	i	ii	iii	iv
(D)	ii	iii	iv	i

(35) Match the following:

List – I	**List – II**
(a) Herbert Hicks	(i) The Elements of Administration
(b) F.W. Taylor	(ii) The Management of Organisation
(c) Henry Fayol	(iii) Scientific Management
(d) Colonel L. Urwick	(iv) Administrative Management

Codes :	**(a)**	**(b)**	**(c)**	**(d)**
(A)	i	iv	ii	iii
(B)	iv	ii	iii	i
(C)	ii	iii	iv	i
(D)	iii	iv	i	ii

(36) **Assertion (A) :** In the study of History, as an academic discipline, a primary source is an artifact, a document, a recording or other source of information that was created during the event or immediately after the event.

Reason (R) : Primary sources are considered as original material or evidences about the topic and are fundamental to history.

Codes :

(A) (A) is true, but (R) is false(B)

(B) is false, but (R) is true.

(C) Both (A) and (R) are true.

(D) Both (A) and (R) are false.

(37) **Assertion (A) :** Indian National Bibliography is the most comprehensive source of Indian publications

Reason (R) : National Library of Kolkata is entitled to receive one copy of each Indian publication under Delivery of Book Act.

Codes :

(A) (A) is true, but (R) is false

(B) (A) is false, but (R) is true.

(C) Both (A) and (R) are true.

(D) Both (A) and (R) are false.

(38) **Assertion (A) :** As per the generally accepted principles of construction of statistical tabulation, every table should have a clear, concise and adequate title so as to make the table intelligible without reference to the text and this title should always be placed just below the body of the table

Reason (R) : A statistical table which reflects its title just above the table and supply information about several interrelated characteristics of data makes the table unwield and inconvenient.

Codes :

(A) Both (A) and (R) are true.

(B) Both (A) and (R) are false

(C) (A) is true but (R) are false.

(D) (A) is false, but (R) is true.

(39) **Assertion (A) :** Knowledge Management involves a number of assets and value added to them.

Reason (R) : Knowledge Management is the core activity of information transfer.

Codes :

(A) (A) is true, but (R) is false.

(B) (A) is true but (R) is. partially true

(C) Both (A) and (R) are true

(D) (A) is partially true, but (R) is true.

(40) **Assertion (A) :** According to Horton and Merchant, information is a commodity like other resources.

Reason (R) : Information is a tangible commodity.

Codes :

(A) (A) is true, but (R) is false.

(B) Both (A) and (R) are false

(C) Both (A) and (R) are true.

(D) (A) is false, but (R) is true.

(41) **Assertion (A) :** Reference section in a Library became insignificant.

Reason (R) : The Web. 2.0 services replaces the reference desk services

Codes :

(A) (A) is true, but (R) is false.

(B) Both (A) and (R) are true.

(C) Both (A) and (R) are false.

(D) (A) is false, but (R) is true.

(42) **Assertion (A) :** Newspaper Digests are the best sources of information to get current and authentic information like books.

Reason (R) : These sources are compiles by going through various newspapers.

Codes :

(A) Both (A) and (R) are true

(B) (A) is partially true and (R) is true

(C) Both (A) and (R) are false

(D) (A) is true and (R) is partially true.

(43) **Assertion (A) :** Encyclopaedias have been regarded as the substitute of all categories of reference sources as these provide all types of information.

Reason (R) : Encyclopaedias provide comprehensive information on all aspects which otherwise are scattered in different categories of reference sources.

Codes :

(A) (R) is true, but (A) is false.

(B) Both (A) and (R) are true.

(C) (A) is true, but (R) is false.

(D) Both (A) and (R) are false.

(44) **Assertion (A) :** Chi-square is an important non-parametric test which does not require rigid assumptions in respect of the type of population being studied.

Reason (R) : Since c^2 is a non-parametric test, it requires only the degrees of freedom (implicitly, the size of the population) for using the test.

Codes :

(A) (A) is true, but (R) is false.

(B) Both (A) and (R) are true.

(C) (A) is false, but (R) is true.

(D) Both (A) and (R) are false.

(45) **Assertion (A) :** Information is a commodity.

Reason (R) : Commodity is a marketable item produced to satisfy human wants or needs.

Codes :

(A) (A) is false, but (R) is true.

(B) (R) is false, but (A) is true.

(C) Both (A) and (R) are false.

(D) Both (A) and (R) are true.

Read the passage given below and answer the questions based on your understanding of the passage (Question Nos. 46-50):According to Wikipedia 'social media' is media designed to be disseminated through social interaction, created using highly accessible and scalable publishing techniques. According to search engine partner, the term social media describes media that is posed by the user and can take many different forms. Some type of social media are forums, message boards, blogs, wikis and podcarts. Social media applications include Google, Facebook and You tube. In social media, communication takes place through messages, status updates, voice chats etc. or through photos/videos sharing, games, virtual goods etc. Antony Mayfield in his e-book titled 'What is social Media'? has defined social media as online media, which encourages contributions and feedback from everyone who is interested, is open to feedback and participation, is a two way conversation, allows communities to form quickly and communicate to form quickly and communicate effectively to share common interests and thrive on their connectedness. The growth of social media is phenomenal. It is being used by all netizens all over the world to a great extent in all areas including business, government, fashion etc. A research conducted by the Institute for Prospective Technological Studies (IPTS) indicates that high take up of social media application outside formal educational settings provides new opportunities for innovation and modernization. With this growing trend, political leaders have also realized its importance as an effective tool to spread awareness and to reach out their voters. Democratic presidential candidate Barack Obama used it during the Presidential elections. Since then, social media is being highly used by a number of politicians all over the world. Myspace has more than 7100 discussion groups related to politics. According to a survey by manpower, 29% of the companies in America and 20% of companies worldwide have a social media policy. People even update themselves through micro-blogging on every aspect of human life including the natural and human disasters. In China, Twitter became the first media in the world to break the news of the Wenzhou earthquake. Social media is being used in fashion industry as well to generate interest in a brand through publicity across online communities and websites. India is one of the most culturally, linguistically and genetically diverse regions having more than one billion people. It is ranked third in Asia in terms of the internet users and quite a number of them are using social media. In fact, approximately 60 millions to 65 millions netizens in India open most of their time on social media/networking sites.

(46) Who defined social media as 'online media' which encourages contributions and feedback from everyone who is interested?

(A) Wikepedia

(B) Institute for Prospective Technological Studies (IPTS)

(C) Myspace

(D) Antony Myfield

(47) Who used the social media for conversing during recent Presidential Election in U.S.A.?

(A) Jimmy Carter (B) Barack Obama

(C) George Bush (D) John F. Kennedy

(48) In China, which social media became the first media to break the news of earthquake?

(A) Facebook (B) Youtube

(C) Twitter (D) Myzamana

(49) In Asia, which country is ranked third in terms of using social media by the people?

(A) China (B) Pakistan

(C) Japan (D) India

(50) Which social website has more than 7400 discussion groups relate to politics?

(A) Orkut (B) Myspace

(C) Facebook (D) Twitter

ANSWERS

01 (b)	02 (b)	03 (a)	04 (a)
05 (c)	06 (c)	07 (d)	08 (c)
09 (d)	10 (b)	11 (c)	12 (b)
13 (a)	14 (b)	15 (a)	16 (b)
17 (d)	18 (c)	19 (a)	20 (c)
21 (d)	22 (b)	23 (b)	24 (c)
25 (b)	26 (c)	27 (a)	28 (a)
29 (d)	30 (a)	31 (a)	32 (a)
33 (a)	34 (a)	35 (c)	36 (c)
37 (b)	38 (b)	39 (b)	40 (a)
41 (b)	42 (b)	43 (c)	44 (b)
45 (d)	46 (d)	47 (b)	48 (c)
49 (d)	50 (b)		

LIBRARY AND INFORMATION SCIENCE

Paper – III

(1) A Boolean query using only AND and NOT is

(a) Fuzzy query (b) Conjunctive query

(c) Routing query (d) Probabilistic query

(2) In which year Janet (U.K.) was established?

(a) 1957 (b) 1983

(c) 1987 (d) 1989

(3) Who developed Repertory Grid Technique for assessing how the users view the world from their own perspective?

(a) A. Delphi (b) Calvin Mooer

(c) J. Belkin (d) George Kelley

(4) A chart in which some figures are broken down into its constituent parts is

(a) Bar chart (b) Column chart

(c) Pie chart (d) Band chart

(5) OAISTER is an example of digital libraries architecture based on

(a) CORBA

(b) Software Agents Architecture

(c) Federated Database System

(d) Metadata Harvesting

(6) RSS feed is a tool of

(a) Web 2.0 (b) Web 1.0

(c) Web 3.0 (d) Graphic Design

(7) The use of more words or symbols that are necessary to convey a meaning results in

(a) Efficiency (b) Accuracy

(c) Redundancy (d) Precision

(8) A rubber stamp impressed on the verso of title page giving information concerning the records and processing of each individual book acquired is called

(a) Book stamp (b) Process stamp

(c) Data stamp (d) Accession stamp

(9) Ontology is

(a) A Documentation service

(b) An Indexing method

(c) Classification of Internet based documents

(d) Cataloguing of Internet based documents

(10) In colon classification, which mnemonic is displayed in the use of digit '4' as for pathology, disease, transport, hybrid etc. ?

(a) Seminal (b) Systematic

(c) Scheduled (d) Alphabetical

(11) Name the similarity measure in which similarity of a document is adjusted such that the similarity of a document to itself is 1.

(a) Cosine measure

(b) Distance measure

(c) Swet's measure

(d) Normalised similarity measure

(12) Which law states that "An information retrieval system will tend not to be used whenever it is more painful and troublesome for a customer to have information than for him not to have it"?

(a) Bradford's law (b) Mooer's Law

(c) Ziff's Law (d) Lotka's Law

(13) Who is the compiler of Web-Bibliography of Rabindranath Tagore?

(a) Bengal Library Association

(b) RRRLF

(c) National Library of India

(d) IASLIC

(14) Who are the publisher of 'Year Book on Human Rights'?

(a) United nations

(b) Ministry of Law, Govt. of India

(c) Europa Publishers

(d) R.R. Bowker

(15) ASTINFO stands for

(a) Asian Scientific and Technological Information Network

(b) Association of Scientific and Technological Information Scientists in Asia

(c) International Network for Exchange of Science and Technology Information

(d) Regional Network for the Exchange of Information and Experience in Science and Technology in Asia and the Pacific

(16) IFLA's programme for capacity building of library associations is named as

(a) BSLA (b) ALP

(c) CLM (d) PAC

(17) The measure of certainty predictability is called as

(a) Entropy (b) Feedback

(c) Redundancy (d) Distortion

(18) A characteristic in which information tends to leak and the more it leaks, the more we have, is

(a) Synergetic characteristics

(b) Diffusive characteristics

(c) Compressible characteristics

(d) Shareable characteristics

(19) Which of the following organizations are associated with the concept of '1000 crore plan to link 9000 libraries in India'?

(i) National Library of India

(ii) National Mission on Libraries

(iii) INFLIBNET

(iv) RRRLF

Codes:

(A) (ii) and (iii) are correct.

(B) (iii) and (iv) are correct.

(C) (i) and (iv) are correct.

(D) (ii) and (iv) are correct.

(20) Which of the following are the core content of ISI web of knowledge?

(i) Current Contents

(ii) ISI proceedings

(iii) Derwent Information Index

(iv) AGRICOLA

Codes:

(A) (i), (iv) and (iii) (B) (i), (ii) and (iii)

(C) (ii), (iii) and (iv) (D) (i), (ii) and (iv)

(21) Which of the following are value added information services?

(i) Aggregator Service

(ii) Referral Service

(iii) Document Delivery Service

(iv) Research Reports/Market Survey Reports

Codes:

(A) (i) and (iii) are correct.

(B) (ii) and (iv) are correct.

(C) (ii) and (iii) are correct.

(D) (i) and (iv) are correct.

(22) Identify the methods used for plagiarism detection:

(i) Term occurrence analysis

(ii) API Testing

(iii) Citation-based plagiarism detection

(iv) Local similarity assessment

Codes:

(A) (i), (ii) and (iv) are correct.

(B) (i), (iii) and (iv) are correct.

(C) (ii), (iii) and (iv) are correct.

(D) (i), (ii) and (iii) are correct.

(23) Which of the following are the main role operators of PRECIS?

(i) Key System (ii) Action

(iii) Performer of action (iv) Form of Document

Codes:

(A) (i), (ii) and (iii) (B) (ii), (i) and (iv)

(C) (i), (iii) and (iv) (D) (ii), (iii) and (i)

(24) Which of the following are the advantages of RFID technology in libraries?

(i) Tags can be read inside a case.

(ii) Hundred of tags can be read at a time.

(iii) Cheaper than Barcode

(iv) Mode security and privacy

Codes:

(A) (i) and (iii) are correct.

(B) (i) and (ii) are correct.

(C) (ii) and (iii) are correct.

(D) (iii) and (iv) are correct.

(25) Which of the following are not change management models?

(i) Kurtlewin's Model (ii) Beer's Model

(iii) Lasswell's Model (iv) Epidemic Model

Codes:

(A) (i) and (iii) are correct.

(B) (ii) and (iii) are correct.

(C) (iii) and (iv) are correct.

(D) (ii) and (iv) are correct.

(26) Which of the following are the International Cooperative Serials Control Program?

(i) CONSER (ii) BIBCO

(iii) SERLINE (iv) CATLINE

Codes:

(A) (i) and (ii) are correct.

(B) (ii) and (iii) are correct.

(C) (i) and (iii) are correct.

(D) (ii) and (iv) are correct.

(27) Which of the following are called 'path finders' to the literature?

(i) Bibliography (ii) Catalogue

(iii) Shelf List (iv) Indices and Abstracts

Codes:

(A) (i) and (ii) are correct.

(B) (i), (ii) and (iv) are correct.

(C) (i) and (iv) are correct.

(D) (ii) and (iii) are correct.

(28) Which of the following facilitate informal communication on the web?

(i) Split Screens (ii) Chat

(iii) Wikis (iv) RSS feeds

Codes:

(A) (i) and (iii) are correct.

(B) (ii) and (iii) are correct.

(C) (iii) and (iv) are correct.

(D) (i) and (ii) are correct.

(29) Which of the following associations have sponsored the Text Encoding Initiatives (TEI)?

(i) ACL (ii) ACRL

(iii) ALLC (iv) ACH

Codes:

(A) (i), (ii) and (iii) are correct.

(B) (ii), (iii) and (iv) are correct.

(C) (i), (iv) and (ii) are correct.

(D) (i), (iii) and (iv) are correct.

(30) Which of the following are limitations of digital libraries?

(i) Full text searching (ii) Operational costs

(iii) Rights management (iv) Hyper text linking

Codes:

(A) (ii), (iii) and (iv) are correct.

(B) (ii), (iii) are correct.

(C) (i) and (iv) are correct.

(D) (i) and (iv) are correct.

(31) The sources of hypothesis, as enunciated by P.V. young are

(i) Genealogy (ii) Culture

(iii) Experiment (iv) Analogy

Codes:

(A) (i), (ii) and (iii) are correct.

(B) (i), (iii) and (iv) are correct.

(C) (i), (ii) and (iv) are correct.

(D) (ii), (iii) and (iv) are correct.

(32) "Women are more in library profession than men." Identify the variable in the statement.

(i) Men and women are independent variables.

(ii) Men and women are dependent variables.

(iii) Library profession is a dependent variable

(iv) Library profession is an independent variable.

Codes:

(A) (i) and (iii) are correct.

(B) (i) and (iv) are correct.

(C) (ii) and (iii) are correct.

(D) (ii) and (iv) are correct.

(33) Syntematic sampling is

(i) A type of probability sampling

(ii) A type of non-probability sampling

(iii) In which first unit is selected randomly.

(iv) Selected on the basis of specified characteristics

Codes:

(A) (i) and (iii) are correct.

(B) (i) and (iv) are correct.

(C) (iii) and (iv) are correct.

(D) (ii) and (iv) are correct.

(34) Who are associated with the digitization of the collection of Rabindra Bhavan, Vishav Bharati?

(i) RRRLF (ii) C-DAC

(iii) NIC (iv) National Library of India

Codes:

(A) (i) and (iii) are correct.

(B) (i) and (ii) are correct.

(C) (ii) and (iv) are correct.

(D) (iii) and (iv) are correct.

(35) Which of the following are the Pillars of SCONUL Seven Pillar Model?

(i) Recognising Information need

(ii) Locating and accessing information

(iii) Using information technology for assessing information need

(iv) Comparing and evaluating information.

Codes:

(A) (i), (ii), (iii) are correct.

(B) (i), (ii) (iv) are correct.

(C) (ii), (iii) and (iv)are correct.

(D) (i) and (iv) are correct.

(36) Resource Description Framework consists which of the following?

(i) Subject (ii) Thread

(iii) Predicate (iv) Object

Codes:

(A) (i), (ii) and (iii) (B) (ii), (iii) and (iv)

(C) (iii), (iv) and (i) (D) (iv), (i) and (ii)

(37) Arrange the following factors of TQM in the order of their implementation:

(i) Development of Human Resource Management

(ii) Standardization of Work process

(iii) Improvement in Internal Organisation Management

(iv) Quality Management Procedures

Codes:

(A) (ii) (iii) (i) (iii) (B) (iii), (iv) (ii) (i)

(C) (iv) (iii) (ii) (i) (D) (ii) (iv) (iii) (i)

(38) Arrange the following according to their year of emergence:

(i) ADINET (ii) SIRNET

(iii) MANLIBNET (iv) DELNET

Codes:

(A) (i) (iv) (ii) (iii) (B) (iv), (ii) (iii) (i)

(C) (iv) (iii) (ii) (i) (D) (iii) (i) (iv) (ii)

(39) Arrange the following according to their year of origin:

(i) Indian National Bibliography

(ii) British National Bibliography

(iii) Cumulative Bool Index

(iv) Books in Print

Codes:

(A) (i) (ii) (iv) (iii) (B) (iii), (iv) (ii) (i)

(C) (ii) (iii) (iv) (i) (D) (iv) (i) (ii) (iii)

(40) Arrange the following according to their levels:

(i) Canons of Cataloguing

(ii) Laws of Library Science

(iii) General Normative Principles

(iv) Principles of Cataloguing

Codes:

(A) (ii) (iv) (i) (iii) (B) (i), (iii) (ii) (iv)

(C) (iv) (i) (iii) (ii) (D) (iii) (ii) (i) (iv)

(41) Arrange the following according to their year of emergence:

(i) LISA

(ii) Dissertation Abstracts International

(iii) Indian Science Abstracts

(iv) Indian Library & Information Science Abstracts

Codes:

(A) (iii) (iv) (ii) (i) (B) (iv), (iii) (i) (ii)

(C) (ii) (i) (iii) (iv) (D) (i) (ii) (iii) (iv)

(42) Arrange the following according to their year of emergence:

(i) INIS (ii) AGRIS

(iii) NATIS (iv) UNISIST

Codes:

(A) (iii) (ii) (ii) (i) (B) (iv), (i) (iii) (ii)

(C) (ii) (iv) (i) (i) (D) (i) (iii) (iv) (ii)

(43) Arrange in sequence the following Model Public Library Acts/Bills in India:

(i) Model Public Library Bill by M.D. Sen Committee

(ii) Model Public Library Act by S.R. Ranganathan

(iii) Model Public Library Act of ILA

(iv) Model Public Library Bill by working group of Planning Commission

Codes:

(A) (i) (ii) (iii) (iv) (B) (ii), (i) (iv) (iii)

(C) (iii) (iv) (i) (ii) (D) (iv) (iii) (ii) (i)

(44) Arrange in sequence the medium used for 'Virtual Reference' in the order of their progress.

(i) Web form (ii) Ask a Service

(iii) E-mail (iv) Social Networking

Codes:

(A) (i) (ii) (iii) (iv) (B) (ii), (iii) (iv) (i)

(C) (iii) (i) (ii) (iv) (D) (iv) (ii) (i) (iii)

(45) Arrange in order the process of stock rectification and stock verification as suggested by S.R. Ranganathan:

(i) Shecking with charged tray

(ii) Shelf Rectification

(iii) Shelf Checking

(iv) Deciding the Quota

Codes:

(A) (iii) (i) (iv) (ii) (B) (iv), (i) (ii) (iii)

(C) (iv) (ii) (iii) (i) (D) (ii) (iv) (i) (iii)

(46) Match the following:

List – I	**List – II**
(a) Qutdated Information	(i) Information Diffusion
(b) Condensed Information	(ii) Obsolete Information
(c) Message	(iii) Compressible Information
(d) Vintage model	(iv) Understanding

Codes :	**(a)**	**(b)**	**(c)**	**(d)**
(A)	iv	iii	ii	i
(B)	i	ii	iv	iii
(C)	iii	iv	ii	i
(D)	ii	iii	iv	I

(47) Match the following :

List – I	**List – II**
(a) Technique for identifying the theme of a document	(i) Cataloguing

(b) Prussian Instruction (ii) Standard for encoding data on CD-ROM

(c) ISO-9960 (iii) Data Transmission Speed

(d) Baud (iv) Bibliographic coupling

Codes :	**(a)**	**(b)**	**(c)**	**(d)**
(A)	iv	i	ii	iii
(B)	i	ii	iii	iv
(C)	ii	iii	iv	i
(D)	iii	ii	i	iv

(48) Match the following :

List – I	**List– II**
(a) Maurice B.Line	(i) Resource Management in Academic Libraries
(b) David Baker	(ii) Planning Academic and Research Library Buildings
(c) Peter Brophy	(iii) Academic Library Management
(d) K.D. Metcalf	(iv) The Academic Libraries

Codes :	**(a)**	**(b)**	**(c)**	**(d)**
(A)	iii	i	iv	ii
(B)	i	ii	iii	iv
(C)	iv	i	ii	iii
(D)	ii	iii	i	iv

(49) Match the following :

List – I	**List– II**
(a) Digital Library	(i) Collections are stored in electronic media formats and accessible via computers
(b) Hybrid library	(ii) Assess to electronic information in a variety of remote

			locations through a local online catalogue or other gateway
(c)	Virtual Library	(iii)	Provides services in a mixed mode electronic and paper environment
(d)	Electronic Library	(iv)	Collection of electronic resources that provides direct/ indirect access to a systematically organized collection of digital objects.

Codes :	**(a)**	**(b)**	**(c)**	**(d)**
(A)	iv	iii	ii	i
(B)	i	iii	iv	ii
(C)	iii	i	ii	iv
(D)	ii	ii	i	iii.

(50) Match the following:

	List – I		**List– II**
(a)	Survey of requirements	(i)	Design phase
(b)	Determining cost efficiency and effectiveness	(ii)	Installation phase
(c)	Review of the programs and their goals	(iii)	Analysis phase
(d)	Complete change over basics of system	(iv)	Evaluation phase

Codes :	**(a)**	**(b)**	**(c)**	**(d)**
(A)	i	ii	iii	iv
(B)	ii	iii	iv	i
(C)	iii	iv	i	ii
(D)	iv	i	ii	iii.

(51) Match the following:

	List – I	List– II
(a)	Nadir Ascending	(i) Hypothesizing
(b)	Ascending to Zenith	(ii) Verification
(c)	Zenith to Descending	(iii) Deductive
(d)	Descending to Nadir	(iv) Empirical

Codes :	(a)	(b)	(c)	(d)
(A)	i	iii	ii	iv
(B)	ii	iv	i	iii
(C)	iii	i	iv	ii
(D)	iv	i	iii	ii.

(52) Match the following characteristics of DBMS with respective activity:

	List – I	List– II
(a)	Reduction of redundancy	(i) Encryption
(b)	Data sharing	(ii) Centralized control
(c)	Data sharing	(iii) No. of application programs
(d)	Data security	(iv) Accurate and consistent data

Codes :	(a)	(b)	(c)	(d)
(A)	ii	iii	iv	i
(B)	iv	iii	ii	i
(C)	iii	iv	i	ii
(D)	i	ii	iv	iii.

(53) Match the following:

	List – I	List– II
(a)	XML	(i) Joe Becker
(b)	METS	(ii) Defence Organizations
(c)	UNICODE	(iii) W3C
(d)	Cryptography	(iv) Library of Congress

Codes :	**(a)**	**(b)**	**(c)**	**(d)**
(A)	i	ii	iii	iv
(B)	iii	iv	i	ii
(C)	ii	iii	iv	i
(D)	iv	i	ii	iii.

(54) Match the following:

List – I	**List– II**
(a) Social Microscope	(i) Cluster Technique
(b) Fundamental Research	(ii) No control over variance
(c) Ex-post facto research	(iii) Case study method
(d) Multi random sampling	(iv) Knowledge for knowledge sake

Codes :	**(a)**	**(b)**	**(c)**	**(d)**
(A)	i	ii	iii	iv
(B)	iii	iv	ii	i
(C)	ii	iii	i	iv
(D)	iv	i	ii	iv.

(55) Match the following:

List – I	**List– II**
(a) Estimation of future expenditure on the basis of previous year expenditure	(i) Programme
(b) Rs. 15 per student and Rs. 200/-	(ii) Comparison
(c) 6.5 %-10% of university budget for the development library	(iii) Per capita
(d) Activities to be accomplished by the library	(iv) Proportional

Codes :	**(a)**	**(b)**	**(c)**	**(d)**
(A)	iv	iii	ii	i
(B)	i	iii	iv	ii
(C)	iii	i	ii	iv
(D)	ii	ii	i	iii.

(56) Match the following:

List – I		**List– II**	
(a)	Identification of user categories	(i)	Market positioning
(b)	Prioriting user groups and services	(ii)	Segmentation
(c)	Information seeking behavior of users	(iii)	Marketing Mix
(d)	Product, price, place, promotion	(iv)	Consumer analysis

Codes :	**(a)**	**(b)**	**(c)**	**(d)**
(A)	i	ii	iii	iv
(B)	ii	i	iv	iii
(C)	iii	iv	i	ii
(D)	iv	iii	ii	i.

(57) Match the following:

List – I		**List– II**	
(a)	FRBR	(i)	Paul Otlet
(b)	POPSI	(ii)	IFLA
(c)	UDC	(iii)	G. Bhattacharya
(d)	www	(iv)	Tem Berners-Lee

Codes :	**(a)**	**(b)**	**(c)**	**(d)**
(A)	ii	i	iii	iv
(B)	ii	iii	i	iv
(C)	ii	iv	i	iii
(D)	iv	ii	iii	i

(58) Match the following :

List – I	List– II
(a) Index Translationum	(i) NISCAIR
(b) Translation Register Index (RT-I)	(ii) NTC, Chicago
(c) World Trans Index	(iii) UNESCO
(d) Common-wealth Index of Unpublished Translations	(iv) ITC, Delft, Netherlands ASLIB

Codes :	**(a)**	**(b)**	**(c)**	**(d)**
(A)	ii	iii	i	iv
(B)	iii	ii	iv	i
(C)	v	iii	i	ii
(D)	iv	ii	v	iii.

(59) Match the following evaluation criteria of print materials:

List – I	List– II
(a) Authority	(i) Typography
(b) Scope	(ii) Stated purpose
(c) Format	(iii) Publisher's reputation
(d) Arrangement	(iv) Cross references

Codes :	**(a)**	**(b)**	**(c)**	**(d)**
(A)	ii	iii	i	iv
(B)	i	iv	ii	iii
(C)	iii	ii	i	iv
(D)	iii	iv	ii	i.

(60) Match the following:

List – I	List– II
(a) Measure of similarity between two documents	(i) Proportion of coefficient association

(b)	Similarity measure based on overlap in terms between two documents	(ii)	Rectangular distance coefficient
(c)	Document similarity based solely on the occurrence of words	(iii)	Coefficient of association
(d)	Similarity measure which is based on the city block distance between two documents	(iv)	Lexical similarity

Codes :	**(a)**	**(b)**	**(c)**	**(d)**
(A)	i	iii	ii	iv
(B)	iii	i	ii	iv
(C)	iii	i	iv	ii
(D)	ii	iii	iv	i.

(61) Match the following authors with their statements on information characteristics:

	List – I		**List– II**
(a)	Peter Drucker	(i)	Human and shareable
(b)	Borlando Cleveland	(ii)	Quantity, Quality, Life
(c)	K.J. McGarry	(iii)	Natural and man-made physical resources
(d)	Williams	(iv)	Resources by analogy with classic resources of labour

Codes :	**(a)**	**(b)**	**(c)**	**(d)**
(A)	iii	i	iv	ii
(B)	iii	ii	i	iv
(C)	i	iii	iv	ii
(D)	i	iv	ii	iii.

(62) Match the following:

	List – I		List– II
(a)	Saraswati mahal Library, Tanjavur (1535)	(i)	Lord Curzon
(b)	Khuda baksh oriental Public Library, Patna (1876)	(ii)	Telugu Nayakas
(c)	Library of Asiatic Society of Bengal (1784)	(iii)	Maulana M.B. Khan
(d)	Imperial Library, Calcutta (1901)	(iv)	William Jones

Codes :	**(a)**	**(b)**	**(c)**	**(d)**
(A)	iii	ii	iv	i
(B)	ii	iii	i	iv
(C)	ii	iii	iv	i
(D)	iii	ii	i	iv.

(63) **Assertion (A) :** With the introduction of Internet, need for reference librarians has been minimised to fulfil the users reference needs.

Reasons (R) : FAQ facility on internet is substituting the need for human interface in libraries.

Codes :

(a) Both (A) and (R) are partially true.

(b) Both (A) and (R) are true

(c) Both (A) and (R) are false

(d) (A) is true but (R) false

(64) **Assertion (A) :** Approaches to Research is not dependent on Epistemologies.

Reasons (R) : Scientific research relies on the application of the scientific method.

Codes :

(a) Both (A) and (R) are true
(b) Both (A) and (R) are false
(c) (A) is true but (R) false
(d) (R) is true (A) is false

(65) **Assertion (A) :** According to the Third Law of Librarianship given by Michael Gorman, we need to use technology intelligently to enhance service.

Reasons (R) : Technology is used to solve problems and improve services and achieve cost-effectiveness rather than adopted for its own sake.

Codes :

(a) (A) iS true, but (R) is false.
(b) Both (A) and (R) are true, but (R) is not correct explanation of (A).
(c) Both (A) and (R) are false
(d) Both (A) and (R) are true

(66) **Assertion (A) :** All reference sources provide uptodate information in their respective categories.

Reasons (R) : As these are compiled from primary sources of information

Codes :

(a) Both (A) and (R) are true
(b) Both (A) and (R) are false
(c) (A) is false but (R) is partially true
(d) (A) is true (R) is false

(67) **Assertion (A) :** The hierarchy based classification schemes have a major role in the organization of the web.

Reasons (R) : The 'hotlists' retrieved by robots based search engines use the technique of relevance of subject descriptors.

Codes :

(a) (A) iS true, but (R) is false.

(b) (A) is false but (R) is TRUE

(c) Both (A) And (R) Are Correct

(d) Both (A) and (R) are wrong.

(68) **Assertion (A) :** Performance Based Budgeting demands that the objectives and goals of agency be clear and performance measures and target to put in place.

Reasons (R) : The key to success firmly rely upon its clear sense of mission and objectives which the funding agencies have proposed to reach them.

Codes :

(a) (A) is true but (R) is false

(b) (A) is false, but (R) is true

(c) Both (A) and (R) are true

(d) Both (A) and (R) are false

(69) **Assertion (A) :** Majority of University Libraries in India are not fully automated.

Reasons (R) : University Libraries in India are meddling with automation of circulation activities.

Codes :

(a) (A) is true but (R) is false

(b) (A) is false but (R) is true

(c) Both (A) and (R) are true

(d) Both (A) and (R) are false

(70) **Assertion (A) :** Mean, median and mode are the simple techniques to get exact averages for data analysis in research.

Reasons (R) : These are the well accepted statistical techniques of research for data analysis of historical data.

Codes :

(a) (A) is false but (R) is true

(b) Both (A) and (R) are true

(c) (A) is true but (R) is false

(d) Both (A) and (R) are false

(71) **Assertion (A) :** Online Reference Service can be offered using IMs. SMs, VoIP, Video, Blogs, Websites and host of such other, mechanisms.

Reasons (R) : Majority of academic libraries in India are equipped with requires infrastructure.

Codes :

(a) Both (A) and (R) are true

(b) (A) is true but (R) is false

(c) (A) is false but (R) is true

(d) Both (A) and (R) are false

(72) **Assertion (A) :** Semantic web is an extension of www in which web contents cannot be expressed in natural language.

Reasons (R) : Semantic web can be easily associated with spider web.

Codes :

(a) Both (A) and (R) are false

(b) (A) is true but (R) is false

(c) Both (A) and (R) are true

(d) (A) is false but (R) is true

(73) **Assertion (A) :** BIOS is a set of programs that handles startup operations in a computer such as power on, self tested and low level control for hardware.

Reasons (R) : The graphical display at the beginning of the program prolongs the life of monitor

Codes :

(a) Both (A) and (R) are true

(b) (A) is false but (R) is true

(c) Both (A) and (R) are false

(d) (A) is true but (R) is false

(74) **Assertion (A) :** For providing an effective reference service, best & up to date reference collection is not as important as is the competent reference librarian.

Reasons (R): An efficient reference librarian can serve the users more effectively even in the absence of best reference collection.

Codes :

(a) (A) is true but (R) is false

(b) Both (A) and (R) are true

(c) (A) is false but (R) is true

(d) Both (A) and (R) are false

(75) **Assertion (A) :** India's contribution to LIS literatures is decreasing.

Reasons (R) : Authors find it more convenient to get their articles published in open access journals.

Codes :

(a) Both (A) and (R) are true

(b) (A) is false but (R) is true

(c) Both (A) and (R) are false

(d) (A) is true but (R) is false

ANSWERS

1 (b)	2 (b)	3 (d)	4 (c)
5 (d)	6 (a)	7 (c)	8 (d)
9 (c)	10 (a)	11 (d)	12 (b)
13 (b)	14 (a)	15 (d)	16 (a)
17 (c)	18 (b)	19 (d)	20 (b)
21 (d)	22 (b)	23 (a)	24 (b)

25 (c)	26 (c)	27 (c)	28 (d)
29 (d)	30 (b)	31 (c)	32 (a)
33 (a)	34 (a)	35 (b)	36 (b)
37 (d)	38 (b)	39 (b)	40 (d)
41 (c)	42 (b)	43 (b)	44 (c)
45 (b)	46 (d)	47 (a)	48 (a)
49 (a)	50 (c)	51 (d)	52 (a)
53 (b)	54 (b)	55 (a)	56 (b)
57 (b)	58 (b)	59 (c)	60 (c)
61 (a)	62 (c)	63 (a)	64 (a)
65 (d)	66 (c)	67 (a)	68 (c)
69 (c)	70 (c)	71 (b)	72 (a)
73 (d)	74 (b)	75 (b)	

12
Practice Papers

PAPER-I

(1) Who was the chairman of the committee on National network system for university libraries

(a) Prof Yashpal (b) R.C. Molhotra

(c) A.B. Lal (d) Sir Fayzee

(2) Grapevine communication is called for

(a) Formal communication

(b) Informal communication

(c) Distance communication

(d) Network communication

(3) Hoover commission Report is related to

(a) Performance budgeting

(b) Program budgeting

(c) Zero based budgeting

(d) Formula budgeting

(4) Which Mughal King is known for setting up a library in Agra

(a) Babar (b) Akbar

(c) Humayun (d) Aurangjeb

(5) CORD stands for

(a) Communication oriental research and development
(b) Centre for occupation research and development
(c) Control on research and development
(d) Centre for oriental research and development

(6) DAISY stands for
(a) Digital Accessible Information system
(b) Development of Analog information system
(c) Digital Archive Inf. System
(d) Digital Access Interaction system

(7) World cat name is given in 2010 to
(a) World library of cat information
(b) World Information system
(c) Union catalog of OCLC
(d) British library lending division

(8) Who is the Head of DRTC
(a) MN Prasad (b) ARD Prasad
(c) C Krashnamurthy (d) MA Gopinath

(9) First Inter library loan code was prepared by
(a) SLA (b) LA
(c) ALA (d) OCLC

(10) In this year DELNET established in India
(a) 1988-89 (b) 1991-92
(c) 1994-95 (d) 2001-2002

(11) What is BUBL link
(a) Catalogue of Internet resource
(b) Catalogue of British library
(c) Catalogue of Web sites of libraries
(d) Gateway of Public libraries

(12) Sher Singh and Bhavana Singh are the editors of

(a) Indian Books in print 2007
(b) Indian Books in print 1864
(c) Cumulative book Index
(d) List of library books

(13) DIALOG was completed in 1966 under the direction of
(a) Roger K Summit (b) Roger R Semons
(c) Royer S Sumit (d) Williom Duglus

(14) BRS online system stands for
(a) Bibliographic reference service
(b) Bibliographic reference system
(c) Bibliographic retrieval service
(d) Bibliographic resource service

(15) Mccolvin's demand theory relates to
(a) Cataloguing
(b) Principle of classification
(c) Book selection
(d) Stock verification

(16) The idea of Bureaucretic school of thought was introduced by
(a) Max weber (b) F.W. Taylor
(c) H.Fayol (d) Gullick and Urwick

(17) Publisher Weekly is the publication of
(a) H.W. Wilson (b) ALA
(c) R.R. Bowker (d) LA

(18) Relate the following classification scheme with their origin year
(a) Rider's international classification (i) 1904
(b) Library of congress (ii) 1934
(c) Subject classification (iii) 1906
(d) Bibliographic classification (iv) 1961

	A	B	C	D
(a)	I	III	II	IV
(b)	IV	I	III	II
(c)	III	I	IV	II
(d)	II	I	III	IV

(19) Arrange the following according to their year of enactment in increasing order

(i) Communication Bill

(ii) Copy right act original

(iii) Information Patent Act

(iv) Software copy right Act

	A	B	C	D
(a)	I	II	III	IV
(b)	II	IV	III	I
(c)	II	III	IV	I
(d)	IV	I	II	III

(20) What is KHOJ

(a) A name of Google

(b) Search engine of Indian Information

(c) A periodical

(d) Name of a software

(21) Which is oldest search engine

(a) Altavista (b) Northern light

(c) Yahoo (d) Google

(22) Universal copyright convention is developed by

(a) DRTC (b) ASLIB

(c) WIPO (d) UNESCO

(23) What is OAISter

(a) Union catalogs

(b) Software for university library

(c) Name of a fish

(d) Management institute

(24) Prolegomena written by

(a) P.N. Kaula (b) S.R. Ranganathan

(c) W.C. Berwick Sayers(d) Margret Mann

(25) Prolegomen IIIrd edition published in

(a) 1937 (b) 1957

(c) 1967 (d) 1977

(26) In CC7 the Notation for Nepal is

(a) 44a75 (b) 44Q7

(c) 441 (d) 44T

(27) If you want to know development in your choice of website by e-mail account

(a) Can buy website (b) Can subscribe RSS

(c) Can search website (d) Can provide home address to that website

(28) What is the work of ISBN check digit

(a) Show country name

(b) Show publisher name

(c) Validates the ISBN

(d) Validates only title of book

(29) Who provide ISSN in India

(a) RRRLF (b) NISLAIR

(c) IASLIC (d) ILA

(30) Who is the distributer of CDS/ISIS in India

(a) NISCAIR (b) DELNET

(c) CALIBNET (d) NISSAT

(31) Identity software for library release by NIC, Delhi

(a) ALICE for window

(b) LIBMAN

(c) SOUL

(d) BASIS PLUS & TECHLIB

(32) Who is the author of the book "Towards paperless Information system"

(a) F.W. Lancaster (b) Calvin Moorse

(c) William Fredrick (d) Max Waber

(33) Identify first commercial on line database service

(a) BRS (b) SDC

(c) DIALOG (d) R.R. Wowker

(34) The word institution is added to IFLA's full name in the year of

(a) 1972 (b) 1974

(c) 1976 (d) 1978

(35) Provide chronological sequence of the following library act according to their enactment in their state

(A) Arunachal Pradesh Public Library Act

(B) West Bengal Public Library Act

(C) Manipal Public Library Act

(D) Uttar Pradesh Public Library Act

(a)	A	B	C	D
(b)	B	C	D	A
(c)	C	B	A	D
(d)	A	B	D	C

(36) American Library Association was formed on

(a) 3rd Sep 1876 (b) 6th Oct. 1876

(c) 10th Dec 1876. (d) 14th Nov 1876

(37) **Assertion (A) :** An indexing language is an artificial language as it uses controlled vocabulary

Reason (R) : It provides different relationship between terms

(a) Both (A) and (R) False

(b) Both (A) and (R) True

(c) (A) is true (R) is false

(d) (A) is false (R) is true

(38) **Assertion (A) :** With large collection of documents Recall can be measured properly.

Reason (R) : The proper estimation of maximum Recall for a query requires detailed knowledge of all documents in the collection

(a) Both (A) and (R) True

(b) Both (A) and (R) is not the correct explanation

(c) (A) is true (R) is false

(d) (A) is false but (R) is true

(39) **Assertion (A) :** Library users becoming more technical in using library services

Reason (R) : We are living in a technology era

(a) Both (A) and (R) is false

(b) (A) is true (R) is false

(c) Both (A) and (R) true

(d) (R) is true (A) is false

(40) **Assertion (A) :** In contemporary digital environment, IPR became the focul point

Reason (R) : Due to Increase of Unfair Use of IP

(a) Both (A) and (R) False

(b) Both (A) and (R) is true

(c) (A) is true (R) is false

(d) (R) is true (A) is false

(41) **Assertion (A) :** The development of Institutional Repositories in India is at a show pace.

Reason (R) : This can be attributed to the non-availability of open source software and lack of interest among the LIS professional

(a) Both (A) and (R) True

(b) Both (A) and (R) false

(c) (A) is true but (R) is partially true

(d) (A) is false (R) is True

(42) **Assertion (A) :** RSS is a Web feed format

Reason (R) : Up dated information has become a necessity of people

(a) Both (A) and (R) False

(b) (A) is true but (R) is false

(c) (R) is true (A) is false

(d) Both (A) and (R) true

(43) **Assertion (A) :** Public libraries in India are not technologically advance

Reason (R) : Public is not interested in technology

(a) Both (A) and (R) true

(b) Both (A) and (R) false

(c) (A) is true but (R) is false

(d) (R) is true (A) is false

(44) **Assertion (A) :** DDC and UDC are the scheme used by most of the libraries of world

Reason (B) : People are not interested in CC and SC

(a) Both (A) and (R) True

(b) Both (A) and (R) false

(c) (A) is true but (R) is not correct exploration of A

(d) (A) is false (R) is True

(45) Arrange the following four Quadrant of spiral of scientific method in their logical order

(i) Ascended (ii) Nadir

(iii) Zenith (iv) Decedent

(a)	I	II	III	IV
(b)	IV	I	III	II
(c)	II	I	III	IV
(d)	III	II	I	IV

(46) Arrange the following books in order of their publication

(i) Classified catalog code

(ii) Prolegomena to library classification Ist ed

(iii) Five laws of Library Science

(iv) Colon classification

(a)	I	III	II	IV
(b)	III	IV	II	I
(c)	III	IV	I	II
(d)	IV	I	II	III

(47) Arrange the following principles and canons according to their levels as enunciated by Dr. S.R. Ranganathan

(i) Principles of cataloguing

(ii) General Normative principles

(iii) Laws of library science

(iv) Canon of cataloguing

(a)	I	II	IV	II
(b)	III	IV	I	II
(c)	IV	I	II	III
(d)	II	III	IV	I

(48) Match the following

(A) Web Navigation element	(i) Telecommunication
(B) Shift + Tab	(ii) SQL
(C) Query language	(iii) Hyper link
(D) TELNET	(iv) Select the previous link

	A	**B**	**C**	**D**
(a)	I	II	III	IV
(b)	III	IV	II	I
(c)	IV	I	III	II
(d)	I	III	IV	II

(49) Match the following

(A) Norton (i) DOAJ

(B) Directory (ii) Antivirus

(C) Personal Web Page (iii) Vendor on Internet

(D) Amazon Com (iv) Blogs

	A	B	C	D
(a)	I	III	IV	II
(b)	III	IV	II	I
(c)	II	I	IV	III
(d)	IV	II	III	I

(50) Match the following

(A) N-List (i) Metadata

(B) Dublin core (ii) Standard code

(C) ASCII (iii) Software

(D) UBUNTU (iv) INFLIBNET

	A	B	C	D
(a)	I	II	IV	III
(b)	IV	III	I	II
(c)	I	II	III	IV
(d)	IV	I	II	III

ANSWERS

(1) a	(2) b	(3) b	(4) c
(5) b	(6) a	(7) c	(8) b
(9) c	(10) b	(11) a	(12) a
(13) a	(14) c	(15) c	(16) a
(17) c	(18) b	(19) c	(20) b
(21) c	(22) d	(23) a	(24) b
(25) c	(26) d	(27) b	(28) c
(29) b	(30) d	(31) d	(32) a
(33) c	(34) c	(35) b	(36) b
(37) b	(38) b	(39) c	(40) b
(41) c	(42) d	(43) c	(44) c
(45) c	(46) c	(47) d	(48) b
(49) c	(50) d		

PAPER-II

(1) What is Kobo?

(a) E-book Reader (b) Library software

(c) Management tool (d) Anti-Virus

(2) In classification scheme chronological device provide class number by using

(a) Alphabet of views (b) Epoches of origin

(c) Space facet (d) Empty digit

(3) Gefland Morris recommends

(a) Scientific principle of management

(b) Smallest main library for university

(c) Huge staff for public library

(d) None of above

(4) Which is not a function of personnel management

(a) Job evaluation (b) Tests

(c) Orientation of site (d) Placement

(5) Chambers's Biographical Dictionary Publishes from

(a) New York (b) London

(c) Edinburg (d) Peris

(6) Which source provides the information about the events of a particular year

(a) Hand book (b) Directory

(c) Year book (d) Bibliography

(7) Which species of classification scheme describe the large schedule of past, present and anticipated future with few schedules of common Isolate

(a) Enumerative classification

(b) Almost enumerative classification

(c) Rigidly faceted classification

(d) Almost freely faceted scheme

(8) Relate the following

(a) Aslib Directory (i) UDC
(b) Metcalf, KD (ii) Reference source
(c) + and / (iii) Fusion
(d) Astrophysics (iv) Library Building

	A	B	C	D
(a)	I	III	IV	II
(b)	II	III	I	IV
(c)	III	IV	II	I
(d)	II	IV	I	III

(9) Match the following

(a) Statesman's yearbook (i) Enumerative
(b) Library of congress (ii) Management
(c) Shelf rectification (iii) World cat
(d) OCLC (iv) Macmillion

	A	B	C	D
(a)	I	II	III	IV
(b)	II	I	IV	III
(c)	IV	I	II	III
(d)	IV	I	III	II

(10) The expert system has 3 basic components that are

(i) Knowledge (ii) Inference Engine
(iii) Language (iv) User interface
(a) I, II, III (b) III, IV, I
(c) I, II, IV (d) IV, I, II

(11) DDC 23rd edition released in the year of

(a) 1999 (b) 2001
(c) 2011 (d) 2013

(12) World Book day is celebrated on

(a) 23rd April (b) 1st May
(c) 10 December (d) 14 November

(13) Gyandharshan is a
   (a) Program of Agriculture
   (b) Journal of Education
   (c) Education Channel of IGNOU
   (d) Website of UGC

(14) State Lenin library was the national library of
   (a) Japan (b) Chicago
   (c) Former USSR (d) UKraine

(15) The earliest universities of India are
   (a) Bombay, Andhra-Pradesh, Calcutta
   (b) Calcutta, Bombay and Madras
   (c) Allahabad, Bombay, Culcutta
   (d) Allahabad, Madras, Bombay

(16) Match the following
   (a) UGC Birth (i) Public library
   (b) Education commission (ii) 1953
   (c) Unesco Meniferto 1949 (iii) 1972
   (d) RRRLF Establishment (iv) Dr. D.S. Kothari

	A	B	C	D
(a)	II	IV	I	III
(b)	I	III	II	IV
(c)	III	I	IV	II
(d)	IV	II	I	III

(17) Who has prepared. Union catalogue of social science periodicals in Delhi libraries
   (a) Delnet (b) NISSAT
   (c) NASSDOC (d) DESIDOC

(18) LIBRI a Journal of library science published from
   (a) Japan (b) USA
   (b) Canada (d) U.K

(19) In DDC 19th edition 350 stands for

(a) Sociology
(b) Political science
(c) Public Administration
(d) Psychology

(20) Who has the revision authority of DDC
(a) Library of Congress (b) ALA
(c) OCLC (d) MEDLARS

(21) OJAS stands for
(a) Online Journal Access service
(b) Open Journal Access system
(c) Open Journal Acquisition system
(d) Ocean Journal Acquisition service

(22) It shows the highest level of development in a device technique or scientific field achieved in the particular time
(a) Trend Report (b) State of the Art report
(c) Research steps (d) Committee Report

(23) UGC Infonet 1.0 started on
(a) 1995 (b) 1999
(c) 2000 (d) 2002

(24) Who was the chairman of the committee on national network system for university libraries
(a) A.B. Lal (b) D.S. Kothari
(c) R.C. Mahrotra (d) Prof. Yashpal

(25) Null Hypothesis, term is coined by
(a) William Rozer Fredrick
(b) Ronald Fisher
(c) William Cook
(d) J.C. Robert

(26) ODLIS stands for
(a) Online dictionary for library and information science

(b) Open directory for libraries and information science

(c) Online dialog between libraries and information scientist

(d) Open distance education for library and information science

(27) Which is not related to Delnet

(a) DELNET Blog (b) NECLIN

(c) DELMARC (d) DEL-PLUS

(28) Webinar means

(a) Technology of Website

(b) Conference by using on line service

(c) Calendar of Website

(d) None of the above

(29) Which canon is called master of canon

(a) Canon of Individualization

(b) Canon of preventions

(c) Canon of consistency

(d) Canon of recall value

(30) Web of science is a/an

(a) Websites related to science

(b) Websites related to science & technology

(c) On line citation indexing service

(d) Search engine

(31) Match the following

(a) 2709	(i) Indian railway library
(b) Mosaic	(ii) International standard
(c) Statistical Bibliography	(iii) Web Browser
(d) A.H. Wheeler	(iv) Hulme

	A	B	C	D
(a)	I	II	IV	III
(b)	II	I	III	IV
(c)	III	IV	I	II
(d)	II	III	IV	I

(32) Which is not related to INFLIBNET

(a) Shodhganga (b) Soul 2.0

(c) N-List (d) Library Quarterly

(33) Which is not an open source software

(a) KOHA (b) Doublin-Core metadata

(c) D Space (d) Green Stone

(34) MARC-21 is a joint effort of

(a) SLA, LA, LC (b) ALA, MARBI, LC

(c) LC, CILIP, CLA (d) ALA, ILA, IASLIC

(35) Which one is relate to IFLA

(a) AACR-2 (b) Drupal software

(c) CDS/ISIS (d) IMCE

(36) Relate the following

(a) Vau Madai (i) IPR

(b) C.A. Cutter (ii) Journal of Library Science

(c) Copy Right Act (iii) IFLA

(d) CCF (iv) Dictionary catalogue

	A	B	C	D
(a)	II	III	I	IV
(b)	IV	I	II	III
(c)	II	IV	I	III
(d)	III	IV	II	I

(37) Alternative name entry is a

(a) Book Index entry

(b) Crass reference entry

(c) Cross reference Index entry

(d) Class Index entry

(38) In classified catalogue code if pseudonym is found out-side the sources and real name on title page which name will be written in square bracket

(a) Real Name (b) Pseudonym

(c) Both (d) None of the above

(39) In MS-Word 2003 Mail merge option is found in

(a) Edit menu (b) View menu

(c) Tool menu (d) Insert menu

(40) UDC online can be subscribe by

(a) UDC consortia (b) OCLC

(c) Library of congress (d) FID

(41) Which Phase relation is not found in CC 6th revised edition

(a) Bias (b) Influence

(c) Tool (d) General

(42) **Assertion (A) :** In this era most of the libraries are equipped with information technology

Reason (R) : young generation are not interested in using IT equipment

(a) Both (A) and (R) True

(b) (A) is true (R) is not correct explanation of (A)

(c) (A) and (R) false

(d) (R) is true (A) is false

(43) **Assertion (A) :** complete digitalization facing problem in libraries

Reason (R) : IPR is a fundamental right of an author

(a) Both (A) and (R) false

(b) Both (A) and (R) true

(c) (A) is true but (R) is false

(d) (R) is true (A) is false

(44) **Assertion (A) :** Most libraries of the world are using DDC

Reason (R) : It is first scheme of classification

(a) Both (A) and (R) false

(b) Both (A) and (R) True

(c) (A) is true but (R) is not correct exploration

(d) (A) is True (R) is false

(45) **Assertion (A) :** deligation of authority smoothens the functioning of libraries

Reason (R) : Authority is a powerful body

(a) Both (A) and (R) true

(b) (A) is true (R) is false

(c) Both (A) and (R) false

(d) (R) is True (A) is false

(46) Relate the following

(a) Blog	(i) System software
(b) Joomla	(ii) Language
(c) Ubuntu	(iii) Content management system
(d) Pascal	(iv) Personal Diary

	A	B	C	D
(a)	I	II	III	IV
(b)	IV	III	I	II
(c)	IV	I	II	III
(d)	III	II	IV	I

(47) **Assertion (A) :** An Index language is an artificial language as it uses controlled vocabulary

Reason (R) : It provide relationship between terms

(a) Both (A) and (R) false

(b) Both (A) and (R) true

(c) (A) is true (R) is false

(d) (R) is True (A) is false

(48) **Assertion (A) :** In India development of institutional repository is at slow pave

Reason (R) : This situation is due to non-availability of open source software and lack of interest among the LIS professionals.

(a) Both (A) and (R) true

(b) Both (A) and (R) false

(c) (A) is true but (R) is partially true

(d) (A) is false (R) is true

(49) IATLIS is an Association of

(a) Librarian of Public Library

(b) Library and Information science faculty

(c) Special Libraries

(d) Information Scientist

(50) Recall and precision ratio are used in the evaluation of

(a) Reference service

(b) Information retrieval

(c) Bibliographic service

(d) Document delivery service

ANSWERS

(1) a	(2) b	(3) b	(4) c
(5) c	(6) c	(7) b	(8) d
(9) c	(10) c	(11) c	(12) a
(13) c	(14) c	(15) b	(16) a
(17) c	(18) d	(19) c	(20) c
(21) b	(22) b	(23) d	(24) d
(25) b	(26) a	(27) c	(28) b
(29) d	(30) c	(31) d	(32) d
(33) b	(34) b	(35) d	(36) c
(37) c	(38) b	(39) c	(40) a
(41) c	(42) b	(43) b	(44) c
(45) b	(46) b	(47) b	(48) c
(49) b	(50) b		

PAPER III

(1) Who is the producer of Ulrich's periodical directory

(a) R.R. Bowker (b) Asia Publishing

(c) Pro Quest (d) Academic Press

(2) SciFinder is relate to

(a) Chemistry

(b) Library & Information science

(c) Science

(d) Environment

(3) Which one is not an open source software

(a) KOHA (b) Green stone

(c) KHOJ (d) Drupal

(4) What is the meaning of Webinito

(a) Web in Technique

(b) Web from beginning

(c) 3WC

(d) Second generation of Web Technology

(5) Web conferencing is known as

(a) On line chat (b) Seminars

(c) Conference (d) Webinars

(6) Joomla & Drupul is

(a) Name of Digital library

(b) Metadata format

(c) CMS

(d) Languages

(7) In UDC Alphabatical device is used in notation starts with

(a) 8 (b) 9

(c) 92 (d) 93

(8) Common communication format is used in classification tool

(a) Classification (b) Data exchange
(c) Data creation (d) Cataloguing on screen

(9) Massive open on line curses is relate to
(a) Distance learning
(b) Education in France
(c) Education by Television
(d) Education for all

(10) Cataloguing in source experiment was started by
(a) ALA (b) OCLC
(c) Library of congress (d) Ifla

(11) Parry committee is relate to
(a) Higher education (b) Secondary education
(c) Public library (d) Special library

(12) 'Service Before Self' the motto should be of
(a) Cataloguing (b) Classificationist
(c) Librarian (d) Ordinary man

(13) Carol Collier Kuhlthan is related to
(a) Reference service
(b) Information explosion
(c) Information seeking behaviour
(d) Special library

(14) Identify from the following which is not the function of personnel management
(a) Recruitment and selection
(b) Training
(c) Induction
(d) Library committee formation

(15) According to Ranganathan staff formula how many person should be in circulation section for 1500 gate hours
(a) 1 person (b) 2 person
(c) 3 person (d) 4 person

(16) Roberts committee in England & Wales was relate to

(a) Use of cataloguing

(b) Staff formula

(c) Use of computer in library

(d) Reference service

(17) Who said "A professional Bible for Indian Libraries" for the book "Library Administration" by Dr. R.L. Mittal

(a) President Truman

(b) Dr. Ranganathan

(c) DM Cooper

(d) Mr. Kenneth R. Shaeffer

(18) AACR3 is

(a) RDA (b) RDF

(c) ALA Rules (d)

(19) In PRECIS role operator 2 reflects

(a) Action/Effect

(b) Location

(c) Agent of transitive action

(d) Key system.

(20) Vatican code published in

(a) 1908 (b) 1909

(c) 1927 (d) 1929

(21) E-ink technology is used in

(a) Microsoft word (c) E-Reader

(b) Distance learning (d) Coloure T.V. screen

(22) CCF first published in

(a) 1980 (b) 1984

(c) 1972 (d) 1948

(23) Which Institute is providing customized version of KOHA to its member

(a) INFLIBNET (b) DELNET
(c) NISCAIR (d) University of Lucknow

(24) What is full name of OWL
(a) Work outside the library
(b) Library on Wheel
(c) Open wide linguistics
(d) Web ontology language

(25) Relate the following
(a) CC part 3 (i) Webfeed
(b) RSS (ii) Role operator
(c) PRECIS (iii) Modes of formation of subject
(d) Dissection (iv) Sacred books

	A	B	C	D
(a)	I	III	IV	II
(b)	III	I	II	IV
(c)	II	IV	I	III
(d)	IV	I	II	III

(26) Match the following
(a) Latest effective decade (i) Protocal
(b) Z39.50 (ii) AACR2
(c) See Reference (iii) Monographs
(d) ISBD (M) (iv) Colon classification

	A	B	C	D
(a)	IV	I	II	III
(b)	I	II	III	IV
(c)	III	I	IV	II
(d)	IV	III	II	I

(27) The successor of AACR-2 is known as
(a) RDF (b) RDA
(c) AACR (d) AACR New

(28) AACR 2 was based on

(a) ISBD (b) AA code

(c) Vetican code (d) CCF

(29) Relate the following

(a) Shodhganga (i) IFLA

(b) Functional requirement bibliographic description (ii) Mysore University

(c) Vidyanidhi (iii) Dublin core

(d) Metadata (iv) INFLIBNET

	A	**B**	**C**	**D**
(a)	I	II	III	IV
(b)	II	I	IV	III
(c)	IV	I	II	III
(d)	II	IV	I	III

(30) IASLIC is founded on

(a) 3rd October 1955 (b) 3rd September 1951

(c) 13 September 1933 (d) 3rd September 1955

(31) OAI- stands for

(a) Open access information

(b) Open article issueq

(c) Open archive initiative

(d) Open access initiative

(32) Selective dissemination of information is the efforts of

(a) Dr. S.R. Ranganathan

(b) Dr. W.C.B. Sayers

(c) H.P. Luhn

(d) Dr. P.N. Kaula

(33) National institute of science communication has merged with

(a) DRTC (b) CDRI

(c) NISCAIR (d) DELNET

(34) Open Access first introduced in

(a) Bombay university library

(b) Calcutta Public Library

(c) Madras University library

(d) Punjab University Library

(35) Asian Recorder publication place is published from

(a) New Delhi (b) Chennai

(c) Mumbai (d) Hydrabad

(36) Who was the supervisor of Dr. D.B. Krishana first Ph.D. Holder in Library science in India

(a) Dr. WC Berwick Sayers

(b) Dr. EJ Coats

(c) Dr. S.R. Ranganathan

(d) Dr. MA Gopinath

(37) Delhi Library Association is the publisher of this publication

(a) Library Herald (b) Indian Press Index

(c) Index India (d) Library Today

(38) Information and Library Network center is established by

(a) RRRLF (b) NISSAT

(c) UGC (d) NBT

(39) Head Quarter of IFLA is located at

(a) The Hague (b) Paris

(c) New York (d) London

(40) "To provide right book, to the right reader, at the right time" principle of book selection enunciated by

(a) Dr. Ranganathan (b) Drury

(c) JH Shera (d) Melvil Devery

(41) Encyclopedia of library & Information science is edited by

(a) Melvil Dewey (b) Paul Otlet

(c) Allen Kent (d) JS Mill

(42) How many principles are given by Henry Fayol scientific management

(a) 12 (b) 18

(c) 15 (d) 14

(43) Third step in POPSI is known as

(a) Verbal representation

(b) Short display

(c) Display of component

(d) Selection of terminology

(44) Identify odd one

(a) UNITERM (b) SCI

(c) PERT (d) PRECIS

(45) In which of the following Indexing system names of author used a keyword

(a) KWIC (b) KWWC

(c) KETALPHA (d) WADEX

(46) Library classification: Evaluation of a Dynamic theory. Who is the author of this book

(a) HE Bliss (b) RS Parkhi

(c) B Sengupta (d) C.G. Vishvanatham

(47) Chicago Manual of style is used in

(a) Library of congress classification

(b) Reference service

(c) AACR-2

(d) Internet

(48) Full name of association ERIC is

(a) Education Research Information centre

(b) Evaluation of Research Interaction centre

(c) Education resource information centre

(d) English Research Information centre

(49) Standard Deviation is used in

(a) Information service

(b) Research Methodology

(c) Modes of formation of subject

(d) Notation

(50) What will be the correct sequence of following concept related to research process

(i) Analysis of data

(ii) Selection of problem

(iii) Formulation of Hypothesis

(iv) Collection of data

(v) Generalization

(a)	I,	II,	III,	IV,	V
(b)	V,	II,	IV,	III,	I
(c)	II,	III,	IV,	I,	V
(d)	II,	I,	IV,	III,	V

(51) In colon classification (6th Rev. ed.) Sigma (S) notation is use for

(a) Sociology (b) Social work

(c) Social science (d) Book science

(52) RDA Stands for

(a) Resource description analysis

(b) Really data access

(c) Resource direct access

(d) Resource description access

(53) Relate the following

(a) SCOPUS	(i) Asian Recorder
(b) Life of Ravindranath Tagore	(ii) Encyclopaedia Britannica

(c) Current news of election — (iii) Biographical sources

(d) Longest platform of the world — (iv) Database

	A	B	C	D
(a)	I	II	III	IV
(b)	II	I	IV	III
(c)	IV	III	I	II
(d)	III	IV	I	II

(54) Information Retrieval term came into use in

(a) 1970 (b) 1950

(c) 1940 (d) 1960

(55) The term metadata was coined by

(a) Ted Nelson (b) Calvin Moorse

(c) Philip Bagley (d) Thamous Cook

(56) Who was the first chairman of UGC

(a) Dr. Ranganathan (b) CD Deshmukh

(c) D.S. Kothari (d) R.C. Mahrotra

(57) Catalogue word derived from

(a) Latin word (b) Greek word

(c) German word (d) French word

(58) Match the following

(a) RINCA — (i) US

(b) BLAISE — (ii) Philadelphia

(c) ERIS — (iii) Asia

(d) BIOSIS — (iv) UK

	A	B	C	D
(a)	III	IV	I	II
(b)	I	II	III	IV
(c)	I	IV	II	III
(d)	IV	I	III	II

(59) D Space is not using by this institute

(a) INFLIBNET

(b) University of Kashmir

(c) Aryabhatta Research Institute

(d) IIM Lucknow

(60) Establishment year of IGNOU is

(a) 1980 (b) 1982

(c) 1985 (d) 1988

(61) International Nuclear Information system supported by

(a) IAEA (b) FAO

(c) UNESCO (d) WIPO

(62) WIPO Stands for

(a) World Intellectual property organisation

(b) Wide information on periodical

(c) Word information power organisation

(d) World intellectual property office

(63) Identify from the following which are not e-book reader device.

(i) Kindle (ii) Koha

(iii) E-print (iv) Kobo

(a) I and II (b) II and III

(c) III and IV (d) I and IV

(64) Memory card is also called

(a) Imagination device (b) SD/MMC

(c) SD/EEP (d) SD/MMR

(65) OCLC is known as

(a) Ohio college library centre

(b) On line college library centre

(c) On line computer library centre

(d) Off line computer library centre

(66) A digit with ordinal value but without semantic value is known as

(a) Blank digit (b) Gap digit

(c) Empty digit (d) Rich digit

(67) Who is the originator of SCI

(a) William Macfarlane (b) Eugene Gurfield

(c) Derik Austin (d) G. Bhattacharya

(68) MBO Theory is developed by

(a) Peter Druker (b) Malthas

(c) Fayol (d) Gullick

(69) Libri is publish from

(a) London (b) Copenhagen

(c) Canada (d) Chicago

(70) When library association (UK) was formed

(a) 1876 (b) 1877

(c) 1896 (d) 1933

(71) Arrange the following Act according to their year of enactment

(i) Andhra Pradesh (ii) Uttar Pradesh

(iii) Chhattisgarh (iv) Goa

(a) I III IV II

(b) I IV II III

(c) IV I III II

(d) I II III IV

(72) What is copyright infringement

(a) Secure copyright (b) Copyright in foreign

(c) Double copyright (d) Breaking of copyright

(73) i10 Index is introduced by

(a) Google (b) Yahoo

(c) Kobo (d) Index in digital library

(74) World wide web consortia relate to

(a) Language

(b) Subject Indexing

(c) Development of open source standards

(d) Abstracting

(75) What is extranet

(a) Access to intranet out-side premises

(b) Name of reference tool

(c) E-reader (d) Consortia

(76) Library 2.0 allow user

(a) Not to participate in web-site

(b) Creation & updating of content

(c) Follow print library rules

(d) Create online library

ANSWERS

(1) c	(2) a	(3) c	(4) b
(5) d	(6) c	(7) c	(8) b
(9) a	(10) c	(11) a	(12) c
(13) c	(14) d	(15) a	(16) b
(17) d	(18) a	(19) a	(20) c
(21) c	(22) b	(23) b	(24) d
(25) d	(26) a	(27) b	(28) a
(29) c	(30) d	(31) c	(32) c
(33) c	(34) c	(35) a	(36) c
(37) b	(38) c	(39) a	(40) b
(41) c	(42) d	(43) b	(44) c
(45) d	(46) b	(47) c	(48) c
(49) b	(50) c	(51) c	(52) d
(53) c	(54) b	(55) c	(56) b
(57) b	(58) a	(59) d	(60) c
(61) a	(62) a	(63) b	(64) b
(65) c	(66) c	(67) b	(68) a
(69) b	(70) b	(71) b	(72) d
(73) a	(74) c	(75) a	(76) b